RAISING THE VEIL;

OR,

SCENES IN THE COURTS.

BY

BALL FENNER.

EMBELLISHED WITH

PORTRAITS OF POLICE, COURT OFFICERS, &c.

"Above all things, my son, avoid litigation, especially in small matters. If a man meets you in the street, and claims the coat you have upon your back, threatening to commence a suit of law for its recovery, strip it off, and give it to him; lest in defending the coat, you may lose your hat and breeches also."

Chief Justice Coyle's Advice to his Son.

BOSTON:
JAMES FRENCH & COMPANY.
1856.

Stereotyped at the
UNITED STATES FOUNDRY,
41 Congress Street, Boston.
C. HOBBS, PROPRIETOR.

TO THOSE GENTLEMEN,

COURT OFFICERS AND OTHERS,

WHOSE PORTRAITS WILL BE FOUND WITHIN THESE PAGES,

RESPECTFULLY DEDICATE THIS WORK.

THE AUTHOR.

PREFACE.

IF the reader, in glancing over the pages of this work, which has been hastily sketched, and imperfectly written, finds amusement sufficient to while away a leisure hour, and, perchance, to gain some instructions respecting the Courts, Lawyers, Officers, and other *attachees*, in the so-called Temples of Justice; and if any, whose proclivities would lead them to involve themselves in litigation, are benefitted by the perusal of these pages, the object of the author will be accomplished. In stating many facts which will be found in this work, the author's aim has been to adhere strictly to the truth, and give a plain, unvarnished tale, especially where the scenes enacted have come under his own personal observation.

A majority of the community have but an indefinite knowledge, and very limited ideas, of the *modus oper-*

andi of Counsellors, Attornies, Court Officers, Policemen, and others, who hold offices in and about our Court Houses. To give this in detail would fill folio volumes. Happy is the man who avoids litigation, and knows not by personal experience the ramifications of criminal or civil jurisprudence.

AUTHOR.

CONTENTS.

CHAPTER I.

CHAPTER II.

CHAPTER III.

CHAPTER IV.

CHAPTER V.

CHAPTER VI.

CHAPTER VII.

CHAPTER VIII.

CHAPTER XI.

CHAPTER X.

CHAPTER XI.

RAISING THE VEIL;

OR,

SCENES IN THE COURTS.

CHAPTER I.

The Boston Court House—The Architecture and Arrangement of the Building—Introduction to Court Officers and Constables—Cells and Lock-ups in the Cellarage of the "Temple of Justice"—Pettifogging Lawyers in search of Victims—Deeds of Darkness done beneath the Eye of Day—Prostitution and Misery as seen through Iron Bars—The way Pettifogging Lawyers Manage to live—The Unfortunate Countryman—A Friend in Need.

"WHAT building is that?" inquired my uncle Zebedee, pointing with his cane to the huge mass of granite, piled layer upon layer, in Court Street.

"That," I replied, "is the Court House."

"Ah!" quoth he, "there have been strange changes since I last visited this place. The time was, when a building one-quarter the size of that, would have been sufficiently large to accommodate all the Courts in Massachusetts ; but now, I suppose, the City of Boston itself is obliged to employ some six or eight Judges, as many clerks, and fifteen or twenty officers."

"Multiply that number by five, and you will come nearer the mark," was my reply.

Uncle Zeb was a quaint, quizzical, eccentric old fellow, and somewhat of a philosopher, withal. Nothing of the slightest importance passed his observation, and although he usually wore a sombre countenance, his little gray, twinkling eyes, which were almost hid beneath his shaggy eyebrows, would occasionally light up, and in them you could discern the workings of a noble mind, while fun and frolic peeped out at the corners of his eyelids ; and although many winters had passed over his head since he last visited the city which he claimed as his birth-place, he could only here and there point out a place that looked familiar ; the old fellow was near the spot where he, his father, and his father's father, first saw the light of day, but he felt like a stranger in a strange land.

As the old gentleman stood gazing at the Court House, he turned suddenly, at the same time striking his hickory cane upon the sidewalk, and asked, "What style of Architecture do you call that building ?"

"That is what I would learn of you," was my reply

"Primitive, sir, primitive," quoth he ; "you can easily make a miniature model of that building, and I will tell you how to do it. Get two sheets of baker's gingerbread, perforate their sides with holes like unto those of a dove-cot or pigeon-house, set them up edgeways, a few inches apart, set up four sticks of fluted candy at both ends thereof, cover the whole with a sheet of brown paper, for a roof, and you will have an exact model of your far-famed Boston Court House."

"I fear you don't appreciate the talent and skill of Boston Architects," was my reply.

The old man stood for a few moments, apparently in abstract reflections, and then continued:

"Since Boston has become a city, the dwellers therein have claimed for it several titles, viz.: Tri-mountain City—City of the Pilgrims—Athens of America, and how many more I know not, while outsiders call it the City of Fanatics, City of Notions, and such like terms. Now, my dear boy, I have a notion, and if I was a member of your City Government, I would propose, and strongly urge, that those windows on either side of that building, be closed up with the same material of which the structure is composed, and convert the same into one vast Mausoleum, and there deposit the dead of all nations, from the Prince to the beggar."

At this juncture, Uncle Zeb signified a wish to visit the interior of this Temple of Justice. As we entered, an officer passed us, with a bunch of very large keys in one hand, and in the other, several papers or documents.

He descended the narrow stone staircase which led to the prisoners' cells, Uncle Zeb and myself following close in his wake. Hearing footsteps behind him, he turned, and recognizing me, we passed the usual morning salutations.

" Anything rich or interesting, to-day ?" I inquired.

" Not much," was the reply ; " fifteen or twenty drunks, three or four street-walkers, two pick-pockets, one burglar, and I believe there is one minister here, snaked up for committing a rape, or obtaining money under false pretences," adding, *sotto voce,* " I don't care a d—n which."

The ponderous bolt moved easily, when he applied the key to the door which led to the inner cells. We passed through, and the officer unlocked the door of a small cell, in which we found some twenty or more human beings, promiscuously huddled together. Some of them were singing Bacchanalian songs, others sitting upon the wooden benches, covering their faces with their hands, while others still were uttering horrid curses and imprecations, and swearing that they would assassinate the officer that arrested them, if ever they obtained their liberty.

Uncle Zeb raised his hands in holy horror, as he looked into this receptacle, which was, I grant, better suited for a cage to confine wild beasts, than a place to inure human beings, especially those who had committed no crime, save and except the undue gratification of their appetites for intoxicating liquors.

Uncle Zeb ventured to inquire of the officer, why it was that so large a number of persons were crowded together in the same cell?

The officer deigned to reply: "You see," said he, "there are two cells only, one for the men, and one for the women, and they don't have to stop here long; we grind 'em off pretty fast, after we get them up stairs. The 'Black Maria' stands outside, and in less than an hour and a half, most of these vagabonds will find themselves carted off, scot free, and handed over to the fatherly care of 'Capt. Robbins.' Oh, they're a precious set; more than half of 'em have been there before, and they seem to like it, 'cause if they didn't, they wouldn't be so ready and willing to go back again."

The officer then unlocked the door of the cell, and called out five or six victims, some of them respectably, if not well dressed, while others were emaciated, having tattered clothes, and a God-forsaken look.

While the officer was examining his prisoners, and looking over his documents, two men made their appearance, hurrying in through the outer iron door, which was left open; each of them seizing a prisoner by the hand, they commenced talking something after this wise:

"My dear fellow," exclaimed the first, cordially shaking the hand of an Irish bog-trotter, "what's the complaint against you?"

"By jabers! I don't know; may the devil take the spalpeen that brought me to this place."

"You're up for drunkeness, I suppose!"

"Devil a bit of drunk was I; sure, and didn't I go to Paddy O'Murphy's wake, last night, and when some of the *Gorsoons* began to kick up a muss, didn't I rush in, an' sure, to stop the throuble, and let Paddy go into his grave like a dacent man, as he always was, and always will be; an' do you see now, just as I was rushing round at the end of the board on which Paddy was stretched, the whole thing upset intirely, and I found myself lying on the back of poor Pat, when the watchman came in, and dragged me off; but sure I am as innocent as a new born baby."

"Who are those men?" inquired Uncle Zeb.

"Blood-suckers," I replied. "Those are two pettifogging lawyers, let us listen to the second one, who is conversing with a well-dressed man." We approached him, and overheard the following conversation:

Pettifogger. "My dear friend, I can get you out of this scrape, in less than one hour, but you must advance me fifteen dollars, to pay court expenses. If the case goes against you, as I am sure it will, unless you have an able attorney, like myself, to defend you, you will be sent to the House of Correction for six or eight months.

You have acknowledged to me that you was in the Shaker Saloon, watching the game of raffling for geese and turkies!"

"But the officer told me that the offence was only a small fine," replied the prisoner.

"Pooh! nonsense, man, House of Correction, certain; but I can get you clear," returned the pettifogger.

"Five dollars is all the money I have," said the prisoner, with a long-drawn sigh.

"Well," quoth the pettifogger, "give me that, and I will trust you for the balance."

The poor devil handed over to the pettifogger a five dollar bank note, which he seized and thrust into his vest pocket, at the same time making a rush for another victim.

As the officer started with the prisoners, to introduce them to the Police Justice, he turned to me, and said: "If you wish to remain here, with your friend, I will leave the keys in the outer door; when you come up, turn the bolt, and bring them to my desk." Thereupon, officer, pettifoggers, and prisoners, disappeared.

During this time, the reader may well believe that "Uncle Zeb" had not been an inattentive listener, and after their departure, his first remark was, "That officer appears to know you well, and places much confidence in you. How easy it would be for you to take those keys, unlock the cells, and allow every prisoner here to escape."

"Aye," I replied, "he knows me well, for I have been in and about this Court House, at my leisure hours, for upwards of seven years. Now suppose I should unlock those doors, and allow every prisoner here to escape, who would be benefited thereby? Should I? No! because I should probably be arrested within six hours, and myself become an inmate of this dungeon, with bolts secured. Would the prisoners be benefited? No! they would all, probably, be retaken, and when brought to trial, fare much worse than they would, had they not availed themselves of the opportunity. I tell you, 'Uncle Zeb,' that were I myself charged with a crime, and confined within the walls of a prison, and my cell-door should be left open, I question much whether I should leave it, unless I was in a foreign country, and knew nothing of the people, or their laws; because a man that courts investigation, and claims trial, (even though he may be guilty,) when he has an opportunity to escape, does more to prove his innocence, than all the attornies in Christendom can do for him."

The old man mused a moment, and was about to reply, when a loud and piercing shriek issued from the cell where the female prisoners were confined. It was nothing new to me, for I had heard similar outcries many times, and oft, from the same cell; but it startled the old gentleman from his propriety.

"In the name of Heaven!" cried he, "what is that?"

at the same time going to the cell, and gazing through the grates, where he was accosted by a large, robust, but bloated woman, with blood-shot eyes, which showed plainly that "Old King Alcohol" held supreme power over her.

"What are you looking at, 'Old Hoss?'" she shouted. "There ain't no trouble here, on'y old Nell Baker's just fell down in a fit, brought on by the '*tremulous demendous*' or the '*delerious tremendous*,' or *somtin* of that sort. Well, folks as will drink rum, must 'spect to suffer some."

During this harangue of the virago, the poor woman lay writhing on the floor of the cell, her eyes apparently turned in their sockets, and bubbling foam issuing from her mouth. Two or three of the prisoners were attempting to raise her up, while another, a girl of not more than eighteen or nineteen years of age, (who was gaudily dressed, and whose eyes must have become, during the night previous, "a fountain of tears," if we could judge by the stripes or gullies running downward upon her face, washing therefrom the chalk and *rouge* with which it had been covered,) was bathing the temples of the poor sufferer with some water taken from a stone jar, which was daily filled for the use of the prisoners.

There was something peculiarly interesting in the appearance of this young girl, and the questions arose in my mind, why she was there? why confined in a felon's cell, with the lowest of the low, and vilest of the vile? the poor inebriate had partially recovered, and being taken up, and seated upon a wooden bench, she commenced uttering curses and imprecations, intermingled with the most obscene language that could be uttered.

Uncle Zeb was disgusted; he said he felt sick at heart, and proposed to leave what he called the "infernal regions." But just as we were about to start, the officer re-entered with three of the prisoners, and among them was the poor devil who was caught in the "Shaker Saloon."

I spoke to him. and said, "You have been convicted, then."

"Yes," he replied, with a mournful voice, "the Judge fined me two dollars and costs, and the Clerk told me that the whole amount was four dollars and fifty-four cents, and if I had never seen that cursed lawyer, who took from me the five dollars, in your presence, I could have paid my fine and costs, and now been on my way home to my wife and family."

Hereupon Uncle Zeb drew out his old fashioned calfskin pocket-book, and placing a five dollar bill in the hands of the poor victim, he said, "There, my good man, go and pay your fine, and start for home; and if you are ever able to pay me, come, or send to No. 31 B—— Street. Take my advice, keep away from Shaker Saloons, and houses of ill-fame, because the Scripture tells us that the paths which lead to those places, are roads to hell, going down to the chambers of death."

The poor man, with tears in his eyes, took the proffered money, handed it over to the officer, got his discharge, and with many solemn protestations, he assured Uncle Zeb, that within one week, he should be repaid, with interest, he started from those yawning iron gates, which were already opened to receive him.

I am happy to say that this man kept his promise most religiously, and I opine that should he live until his hair becomes whiter than the shirt which he wore on that occasion, he will never again be immured in the cells of the Boston Court House, nor pay money to swindling, pettifogging lawyers.

Of these pests, and cancerous sores, misnomered "Attorneys at Law," who live and fatten upon the hard earnings of the poor, indigent, and ignorant portion of our community, I shall treat more at length in a subsequent chapter of this work.

Uncle Zeb signified his desire to depart, having seen as he said, wretchedness and misery enough for one day. He promised, however, to meet me next morning, at nine o'clock, and visit the court room, where these unfortunate outcasts are brought up for trial, to be condemned or acquitted, according to law and evidence.

As we parted, the old gentleman quietly remarked,

"Surely there is much misery in the world, that ninety-nine persons out of a hundred know not of ; and I hope that in your orisons you omit the sentence, 'Heaven help the rich, the poor can beg.'"

"That is not a part of my petition," said I.

"I am glad of it," he replied ; "but it appears to me that no truly good man, can look upon scenes like these, without mentally ejaculating, Heaven protect the children of poverty and vice, and save them from the clutches of these reckless and unprincipled men, who prowl about the court-houses, and practice at the Bar, in more senses than one."

SETH TOBY, ESQ.

(See Page 103.)

CHAPTER II.

First Impressions on visiting the Police Court Rooms—Organization of the Police Court in Boston—First Justices appointed, and those appointed since that time—Average number of cases daily brought before this Court for trial—The Swindling Attorney—The Common Drunkard—The way a policeman sometimes swears, when under Oath—The unfortunate Night-walkers—The Philanthropist—The advantages of Rouge and a handsome Frontispiece—The Cyprian's Description of the House of Correction—Municipal Court Room—The Hen-Coop built for Prisoners—The Court Crier—Troubles and vexations of a Philanthropist.

THE next morning, at the appointed hour, my Uncle Zeb was ready to accompany me, and make his *debut* in the Police Court room. And here I will give the reader a slight sketch of the Police Court of Boston, from its formation down to the present time.

This Court was organized in the year 1822. The Justices appointed at that time were William Simmons, Henry Orne, and Benjamin Whitmer.

Judge Orne resigned his office in the year 1830, and J. G. Rogers was appointed to fill the vacancy. Judge Whitmer resigned in 1834, and James C. Merrill was appointed in his stead. Judge Simmons died in 1843, and Abel Cushing wanted the Ermine robe, and he got it. Judge Merrill resigned in 1852, and Thomas Russell, (a gentleman of the legal profession, about twenty-six years of age,) was appointed to fill the vacancy. The appointment at that time caused many venerable, superannuated "old Fogies" to roll up their eyes with holy horror, and ejaculate, "God save the Commonwealth." Some of them predicted that in a few years minors would be appointed to offices of trust, honor and emolument, but they were shortly after obliged to acknowledge that the appointment of Mr. Russell to the bench, was a judicious movement, and that he is a fair, impartial and upright Justice.

The year that the Police Court of Boston was organized, Thomas Power was appointed the Clerk thereof, which office he has held up to the present time, (one year only excepted.) We shall speak of the Judges, Clerks and officers, more at length, in another chapter of this work.

Twenty-five years ago, the Police Court of Boston presented a very different appearance from the Court at the present time. Then, three or four cases a day were the average number brought for trial, and, occasionally, when six or seven prisoners were arraigned, the Justices, Clerks and officers, seemed to talk and act as though it was almost an impossibility to get through so many cases in one day. Now, how changed the scene. Instead of five or six cases, we sometimes have between fifty and sixty. I am inclined to think that thirty-five is about the average number. Two-thirds of these cases, at least, are arraigned for rioting and drunkenness, and are very rapidly disposed of. The unfortunates are called up to the prisoners' bar, and sometimes the Clerk will read the complaint to them, and sometimes he will omit it, simply holding the document in his hand, and saying to the prisoner:

"You was brought here for being drunk, last night! Was you drunk?"

If the prisoner says "Yes," the Clerk immediately adds, "The court find you guilty, and sentence you to pay a fine of three dollars and costs, for want of which you stand committed."

Before the prisoner can collect his scattered and bewildered thoughts, he finds himself hurried down stairs, and securely locked up in the cell from which he had been taken, perhaps, three or four minutes previous.

But if the victim says "No!" two or more policemen rush to the stand, with surprising agility, and, raising their right hands, stand ready to swear, as fast as their tongues can wag, that the prisoner was not only drunk, the night previous, but that he was noisy and quarrelsome. If the prisoner has no counsel, the Judge will ask him if he wants to ask those witnesses any questions. The poor, bewildered devil will commence talking, perhaps very incoherently, while the Judge is recording his sentence, and passing the same over to the Clerk; the victim finds himself "booked" for a free ride in a safe and commodious vehicle, which runs regularly every day (Sundays excepted,) between the Court House and South Boston, called the "Black Maria;" and although the prisoner is sure that the State will furnish him with board and lodging, gratis, for three months, not one look of gratitude can be seen in his countenance, while the officer is hurrying him off to the cellarage, there to remain until the Judge shall decide who his travelling companions must be.

When Uncle Zeb entered the court room, it was all bustle and confusion. The Judge had not made his appearance, but the Clerk and his assistants were busily engaged in filling out warrants, complaints, &c., while the officers were looking over their lists of prisoners, and calling out the names of witnesses who had been summoned to appear in the cases which were to come up for trial that forenoon. Shortly after, the Judge came in, and the officer of the day shouted "Court!" The noise and confusion partially ceased, attornies, witnesses and spectators doffed their hats, and one of the officers, with a bunch of keys in his hand, started for the regions below. He soon re-appeared, followed by eight miserable, woe-begone beings, who were ushered in, and seated upon the prisoners' bench.

Uncle Zeb, who had been carefully watching all the proceedings remarked that "this was a disgrace to the city of Boston, a shameful disgrace."

"What?" said I.

"This court room," he replied. "It is a miserable, narrow, contracted, ill-ventilated hole, more suitable for a dog-kennel than a temple of Justice. I thought the Recorder's room in the New York "Tombs" was bad enough, but that is a perfect palace compared with this place."

"We'll not quarrel on that point," quoth I, "but we shall have a larger and a better room by and by."

One of the pettifogging lawyers which we saw the day previous, in the cells below, victimizing the victims, was trying to pick up a subject among the prisoners. He found one, and when the Clerk called the man to the stand, the "sucker" announced himself as counsel for the defendant.

"That man will be convicted, whether he be guilty or innocent," said I to Uncle Zeb.

"What is the charge brought against him?"

"Don't know, nor don't care," was my reply. "If you will just watch the trial, you will see whether I am correct or not."

The complaint against the prisoner was for assault and battery, and the testimony of the government witnesses was very defective, it being almost impossible for them to tell who commenced the affray. But our pettifogger in his cross-examination, elicited from the witnesses the fact that the prisoner was a fractious and ugly man; and when he imbibed too much intoxicating liquor, he would commence a quarrel with his best friends, and "kick up a muss" whenever an opportunity offered.

The Judge reviewed the testimony, imposed a fine of fifteen dollars, together with good and suffiicient sureties in the sum of fifty dollars, to keep the peace for six months, and for want thereof to stand committed. After sentence was pronounced, the pettifogger advised the prisoner to appeal his case, and carry it up to the Municipal Court. He did so. The Judge ordered him to recognize in the sum of two hundred dollars, for his appearance then and there. The man could not furnish the sureties, and was carted off to prison.

"Just as I predicted," quoth I, nudging the old gentleman's elbow.

He shook his head, and simply replied, "It is too bad, it is abominable!"

The rest of the prisoners were quickly disposed of. Some of them were arraigned for simple drunkenness, others as common drunkards; six of them were convicted, one of them discharged.

The discharged prisoner was an elderly man, fifty-five or sixty years of age, and the close observer could see by each look and action, that he was no stranger in the court room. He was complained of as a common drunkard, and his tremulous form showed but too plainly that he had not fully recovered from the previous night's debauch. He plead not guilty, but two police officers swore positively that they had seen the man staggering drunk five or six times within the past two months.

"Do you wish to ask these witnesses any questions?" said the Judge, addressing the prisoner.

"No, your Honor," was the reply.

"Do you wish to say anything about your sentence? If so, I will hear you."

The old fellow's countenance lighted up with a serio-comical expression, as he replied:

"Your Honor, those two policemen have sworn positively that they have seen me drunk five or six times within the past two months; but if your Honor will refer to your books, you will see that three months ago you yourself sentenced me to the House of Correction. My term expired yesterday, and I was liberated. That I celebrated the day by imbibing rather too freely, I am willing to admit, but no man can get drunk on the beverage furnished by Capt. Robbins."

The Judge turned to his book, and found that it was even so. He then ordered the prisoner to be discharged, and at the same time cautioned the police officers to be more careful and guarded, for the future, otherwise he should be obliged to allow a very wide margin in taking their testimony, whenever they appeared upon the witness stand.

The prisoner's bench was again filled with females, who had been arrested for night-walking and soliciting men. Some of them were not more than sixteen or seventeen years of age, but all were the children of crime, prostitution and vice. Some were meanly clad, while others were gaudily dressed, with a profusion of flowers and feathers fastened to their bonnets. Some looked downcast, dejected and forlorn; others, who had travelled longer in the downward path of crime, confronted the gaze of the assembled crowd, with a bold, reckless, brazen look of impudence.

"Who is that fidgety old fellow, whose skin looks like a piece of brown parchment? He's here, there, and everywhere. A few moments ago I saw him wrangling with one of the officers, now he is in earnest conversation with those females," quoth my "Uncle Zeb."

"That," I replied, "is John Augustus, the philanthropist."

"What position or office does he hold in this court?"

"None, that I know of," was my reply.

"Does his philanthropy support him?"

"He could answer that question himself much better than I can," was my response. "I will introduce you to him, by and by; meanwhile, you had better watch his movements."

One of the girls was now called up to the prisoner's stand. She plead guilty to the charges preferred against her.

"I'll bail that young woman for thirty days, your Honor," cried John Augustus. "I know her parents, and very respectable people they are, too. If I can't reform her, I'll bring her into court at the expiration of that time, to be disposed of as you will."

Judge. Mr. Clerk, you may take Mr. Augustus for bail, in the sum of thirty dollars, for the prisoner's appearance here in thirty days from this date."

When the next "unfortunate" was called up, she also plead guilty. One of the wicked reporters was heard to remark, "John won't bail that 'old gal,' she's too old and ugly." The reporter was right. She was sentenced to six months' imprisonment in the House of Correction. Instanter, the fountains of her eyes were opened, and while the waters gushed forth freely, her sobs and boo-hoo's could be heard above the noise within, and the rumbling of express-wagons without the Court House.

The kind hearted Judge was evidently moved by those tears, and addressing the woman, he said:

"The court will give you twelve hours to leave the city. After that time, if you are found within our precincts, or at any time within the six months next ensuing, the sentence already passed will be executed upon you."

Never did the wand of a magician produce a greater

transformation than those words of the Judge, as they fell upon the ear of the prisoner. The salt water ceased to flow from her optics, which were suddenly lighted up, while her countenance was wreathed with smiles.

The Clerk informed her that she was at liberty to depart, and she started, without waiting for a second order or invitation. As she passed John Augustus, she saluted him with an impudent toss of the head, informing him she was under no obligations to him, and hoped to meet him in that uncomfortable place, the exact locality of which has never yet been discovered, but where it is supposed, by some, that tremendous fires are kept up, both night and day.

The balance of the female prisoners were then arraigned; each of them plead guilty, and each of them received precisely the same sentence given the one who had just departed.

"Do you think all those females will leave the city in twelve hours?" asked Uncle Zeb, watching them as they left the Court House.

"Not a bit of it," was my reply. "They will probably change their lodgings; those who reside at the north part of the city will remove to the south part, and *vice versa*. By so doing, you perceive they will not come in contact with the same police officers who arrested them on this occasion; and even if they should, the officers would not probably arrest them, unless they were found following their old profession. But if they are brought into court again, the sentence will surely be executed upon them; even John Augustus himself could not save them. But here comes another, of the same sort. She is complained of as being a common drunkard. I have seen her in this court room several times before.

"What a miserable looking wretch," quoth my Uncle Zeb.

"Aye," I replied, "miserable indeed. Four years ago, that poor wretch was a fine, handsome, fascinating woman of fashion. She belongs to a very respectable family, who reside but a short distance from this city. In an evil hour, she fell into the snare of the tempter. Her parents and relatives discarded her; she took refuge in one of the fashionable brothels which abound in the west section of the city. Her downward course in the path of vice was very rapid, and during the past year she has spent five months in the House of Correction, and the remainder of the time amongst the vilest of characters, in and about a section of the city called the 'Black Sea.' The lawyer who was sitting by your side, and left so abruptly when she was brought into court, *was her seducer!* Such, in brief, is the history of the once beautiful and accomplished Susan K——."

"Uncle Zeb" gazed intently at this wreck of humanity; he fetched a long-drawn sigh, but said nothing.

After the Judge had ordered Susan to the House of

Correction for four months, she impudently inquired, why he didn't give her six? "I know the House of Correction," said she. "We get a pound of bread every morning—see all the ladies and gentlemen that come to bring tracts—pray louder than the parson—make love to the officers—coax 'em to let me out on the Fourth of July—good-by, Judge, I'll call to see you again one of these days!"

The prisoner was remanded to the lock-up.

My Uncle Zeb signified a wish to visit some of the upper courts. I therefore accompanied him to the Municipal Court Room. The scenes here are altogether different from those enacted in the lower court room, although nothing but criminal cases are brought before this court for trial, and probably more than two-thirds of them have been previously examined by one of the Justices of the Police Court. Everything here is quiet and orderly, and however crowded the court room may be, it is seldom you will hear the officers shouting, "Silence in the court!" "Stop talking!" "Go find a seat, or else clear out!" and such like expressions, which are often heard in the court room below. Everything is systematized here. The attornies, witnesses, reporters, &c., each have their seats appropriated, and interlopers but seldom attempt to occupy them. Directly in front of the Judge's bench, there is a large coop or box, with seats to accommodate some twenty-five or thirty prisoners. This box is one of the best models for a hen-coop I ever saw. You have only to nail slats across the top, put in a few poles for roosts, and you have the thing complete. This coop was constructed, under the directions of the County Attorney, the very year that the hen fever raged so terribly. Many supposed that the worthy attorney became slightly affected with the disease, and while constructing a receptacle for prisoners, had a *coop* or *stye* in his eye.

Shortly after we entered the Municipal Court Room, the court adjourned. The Court "Crier," a very gentlemanly and worthy officer, in announcing this important fact, spoke as follows: "All persons—having—Honorable Court—depart—three o'clock—this afternoon—God save—Commonwealthen—Massachusetts." Before the Crier had finished his speech, the Judge had stepped out, the prisoners had disappeared through the side door of the coop into a small room in the rear, where several witnesses, attornies and others, were making tracks for Parker's Saloon, with the laudable intention of moistening the alimentary channel with a modicum of that fluid which, when properly used, maketh glad the heart of man.

My next move was to introduce Uncle Zeb to that worthy and most estimable man, Judge Bishop. After a few minutes conversation, it appeared that they had known each other in their younger days, although they had not met for more than thirty years. The Judge obtained a promise from my uncle that he would dine with him the next day, and they parted, after cordially shaking hands, and giving each other a significant sign, which I did not understand.

As I was passing out through the vestibule of the Court House with Uncle Zeb, we were saluted by John Augustus, and I formally introduced the two venerable gentlemen to each other. John can talk very rapidly, while my uncle is a man of few words and slow speech. John assured Uncle Zeb that he had more business to attend to that afternoon, than any three ordinary men could manage in a fortnight. "I have got to go down to the Jail," said he, "and try and get a woman out who was put in there for selling liquor—her husband was sent to the House of Correction, about three weeks ago, for the same offence—don-no whether I can get her out or not. I must go and look after her children, any way. She's one girl, any way, about seventeen years old, who is very good looking—I don-no whether she is virtuous or not, but I think more'n likely as not she is; but I'll soon find out. Then I've got to go over to Charlestown, and see about a girl there, I bailed out the other day — she's got into some scrape again. I don-no what it is, but I must go and see. And then there's three or four down in the lock-up, that I must look after, and see when"—

How long the philanthropist would have continued this strain, had he not been called away by an officer, I know not.* He invited Uncle Zeb and myself to visit him at his house, some leisure evening, which we promised to do. He left us, and Uncle Zeb returned to his lodgings.

---

* As I intend to give a minute description of *the man*, John Augustus, in another chapter, it is only necessary for me to briefly remark, that those who come in contact with him in business matters, and more especially in matters pertaining to courts, must expect that he will reel off more line from the end of his tongue in fifteen minutes, than any ordinary man could accomplish in four times that space. Those who do not know him, can hardly comprehend his character and style of language, by any description that can be written.

CHAPTER III.

The Philanthropist's Harem—Description of its Inmates—How Pseudo Lawyers are Manufactured—The way they manage to obtain verdicts—Honesty of Lawyers holding high positions—The man who pleads his own cause, does not always have a Fool for his Client—The Judge's Bench, &c., &c.

A FEW evenings afterwards, accompanied by Uncle Zeb, I visited the house of John the philanthropist, whose surname was Augustus. The house literally swarmed with females; and if some of them had been fairer looking, and all of them better clad, a stranger might have been led to suppose that he was in a Sultan's Harem.

We were conducted into a small, well furnished room, and presently John made his appearance. As he came in, he spoke to one of the females, and said:

"If anybody calls for me, I shan't be at home for half or three-quarters of an hour."

He then closed the door, threw himself into an old arm-chair, and that tongue of his, which appears to be hung in the middle, and oiled at each end, was immediately put in motion.

ELIJAH K. SPOOR.

(See Page 111.)

"You haint been in court to-day?" I shook my head. "Thought not—I didn't see you there. Thirty-two simple drunks, seven common drunkards, and eight or ten larceny cases. I bailed out three, and let the rest slide. Didn't believe I could do anything with 'em—afraid to try it, anyhow. Young M—— was brought up for getting drunk, last night. I paid his fine—don-no whether he will pay me or not—guess he will, though. You know him well enough, his father keeps a store up on Cornhill—appears to be a very clever man, but I don-no much about him. I never knew the boy was dissipated before to-day; but you can't tell—most every-body drinks, now a days. Some that pretend to be very temperate, drink the worst."

Here, a woman, who was not very young or beautiful, entered the room, with a note in her hand, which she gave to the philanthropist. He laid it on the table, and continued:

"This is one of my girls. I've had her here nearly a month—must take her into the court, next Wednesday, for sentence. One cent and costs, that's all. Must try and get her some good place to live out. Guess we can reform her, if she don't get in with her old companions again." As the girl left the room, Uncle Zeb remarked:

"I see, Mr. Augustus, you have a large number of females about your house. Are they all the unfortunate children of vice?"

"All but my own family," he returned. "I've got a house full, and I suppose it would be full if it was twice as large."

"And do you really support and provide for all these people, at your own expense?" was Uncle Zeb's next query.

"Well, not exactly," replied John; "there are many charitable people, in the city of Boston, who are willing to give for benevolent purposes, when they know how and for what the funds are to be expended. If a man is taken up for drunkenness, and I pay his fine, and get him discharged, he is almost sure to repay me, as soon as he earns the money. It is very seldom I ever lose anything in that way."

"And what proportion of those females which are taken from houses of ill-fame, and rescued from the prisons, become reformed?" I inquired.

"A great many," replied John. "I don-no what proportion, but suppose one out of ten was reclaimed, would not that be well worth the time, labor and money that is expended on the whole? Do we not read, that he who turns one sinner from the error of his ways, shall save a soul from death, and hide a multitude of sins?"

During our conversation with the philanthropist, the door-bell had scarcely remained quiet for two minutes at a time. It was a constant jingle, jingle, jingle, and I proposed to Uncle Zeb that we had better take our leave, which we did, after being urged to repeat our visit.

After accompanying the old gentleman home, and getting comfortably seated in his cosy sitting-room, the conversation commenced on the subject of "Attornies" and "Counsellors at Law."

"It appears," quoth the old gentleman, "that you do not have a very exalted opinion of your city lawyers."

I replied, "Boston can boast of more distinguished legal gentlemen than any other city in the Union. We have quite a number of attornies that are ornaments to the profession. Those are men who deal fairly and justly with their clients, who will not commence a suit in any case, unless they believe that they have a reasonable prospect of success, except where the client is some wealthy numskull, who wants to spend some four or five hundred dollars to gratify a feeling of malice, or for some other similar cause. It is of the miserable charlatans and impostors, who live by sucking the life blood from the poor and unfortunate, I complain. With many of our most enlightened citizens, it is paradoxical how so many of these pests manage to get admitted to the bar, and thus be allowed to practise in all the courts of Massachusetts. But this query is easily answered.

"I will give you one case, that came under my own observation, which will, with a few slight alterations, apply to hundreds of others. A young man, who resided in a neighboring city, was sent by his father, when he was seventeen years of age, to learn the carpenter's trade. He was not fond of his books or study, although he bid fair to make an excellent mechanic. Before he was twenty years of age, he resolved to lay down the chisel and fore-plane, and become a lawyer. He obtained an introduction to a young practitioner, to whom he agreed to pay fifty dollars, for the privilege to remain in his office for one year, also agreeing to do all writing, copying, &c., which the attorney might require, and in return for his money and services, the lawyer agreed to get him admitted to the bar, to practise in all the courts in the State.

"At the expiration of the year, in glancing over one of the newspapers of the day, I read the following notice: 'In the Supreme Court, yesterday morning, Judge B—— on the bench, on motion of B—— G——, Esq., E—— K——, Esq., was admitted to practise in all the courts in the State of Massachusetts.'

"A few days afterwards, I saw an imposing sign fastened upon a building, in the vicinity of the Court House, lettered, 'E—— K——, Counsellor at Law.'"

Here Uncle Zeb remarked, "Surely the Judge examined the young man, before he was admitted! Did he not?"

"Oh no," was the answer. "The Judge takes it for granted, that the attorney who proposed the candidate, is satisfied, and believes that his *protege* is deeply versed in legal lore. Thus you will perceive that a pettifogging lawyer is easily manufactured. The moment he nails up his shingle, he also will take in a student, upon the same terms, and with the same stipulations which he himself had agreed to and paid, and in this way, pettifoggers increase faster than rabbits."

"In the name of Heaven," cried Uncle Zeb, "how do all these manage to get a living? They must have food and clothing!"

"By robbery!" I answered, "legalized robbery. It would fill a volume to describe all their plans, plots, tricks and machinations. I will give you one illustration, and that will suffice. You will bear in mind that lawyers have but one motto, viz.: 'Diamond cut diamond,' and 'All's fair in our profession.'"

"Not long since a couple of well dressed females entered an attorney's office, and requested him to have the landlord of the house in which they resided, arrested for slander.

"The younger of the twain, a good looking woman, who was, perhaps, twenty-five or six years of age, appeared to take more interest in the case than the other, although her companion was the party slandered, libelled and abused; she having no interest in the matter herself, only to see justice done, and the wrong righted. She assured the attorney that her companion was a hard-working, honest, and virtuous woman, who supported herself and three children, very respectably, by her own hard earnings. She averred that the landlord had stated, before two or three witnesses, that Mrs. M—— was a harlot, kept a disreputable house, and that he should eject her therefrom, forthwith. She also stated that she had known Mrs. M—— for more than three years, and was perfectly satisfied she was a worthy and virtuous woman; that she could bring a hundred witnesses who would corroborate her statements.

" The lawyer rubbed his hands in joyous glee, and assured the parties that this was a good case, an excellent case, and if they would leave with him a retainer's fee of ten dollars, he would proceed to prosecute it, forthwith.

" Here was a serious obstacle thrown in the way. The prosecutor had no money, and the attorney cogitated:—'Wealthy man—witnesses to be relied upon—sure thing—seventy-five dollars, at least—too much to lose—I'll go it!'

" Shortly afterwards, the landlord was waited upon by an officer, who placed a document in his hand, the substance of which was, that his presence would be required in the Justices Court of the city of Boston, county of Suffolk, on Friday, the sixteenth day of June next ensuing. What passed between the defendant and his counsel, I know not; but I do know that both parties appeared with their counsel, on the day of trial. In the interim, the counsel for the defendant had obtained an interview with the principal witness, and when the case was brought up for trial, many facts were elicited, which were entirely unlooked for by the plaintiff's attorney.

"The friend and companion of the plaintiff was called to the stand, and she testified that Mrs. M—— was one of the most abandoned and profligate women that she ever knew in the whole course of her life. She swore that she would not associate with her, nor be seen in her company, under any conditions! The counsel for the plaintiff was taken all aback; he looked at the woman with perfect astonishment, as he commenced his cross-examination.

"'Did you not,' said he, 'tell me that that woman was pure and virtuous, and all that had been reported against her character was a concoction of lies?'

"'I! what, I?' she retorted. 'I never saw you before to-day. I don't know who you are.'

"'Did you not visit my office with this lady' (pointing to the plaintiff, who sat near him,) 'about two weeks ago?'

"'No sir! I am a respectable woman, and never associate with such characters.'

"'How do you know that she is disreputable?'

"'Because I've lived in the house with her six months, and I've often seen strange men in her rooms, both in the day time, and in the night.'

"'Did you not speak to me on the steps of the Court House, this morning?'

"'Yes,' was the reply of the witness; 'you spoke to me, and said, if my testimony was strong, Mrs. M—— would recover damages, and you was a going to divide with her, and you'd do something handsome by me; but I would not listen to your proposals, because I am a married woman, and a virtuous woman, thank God.'

"'Do you know that you are on your oath?' asked the attorney, sharply.

"'Do you take me for a fool, or do you want me to perjure myself?' was the reply.

"The counsel for the plaintiff hereupon arose, and addressed the court as follows:

"'Your Honor, this witness came to my office with the plaintiff, and was very urgent that I should prosecute this suit, assuring me that the plaintiff was a most estimable lady, and had been grossly slandered; and she has either misrepresented the case to me, or she has perjured herself upon that witness-stand.'

"The witness gave the attorney a look of utter contempt, as she remarked:

"'O! you may gas and blow as much as you have a mind to! His Honor would not believe one word you said, even if you should swear to it.'

"Two other females were brought upon the witness-stand, who testified to hearing the slanderous words uttered by the defendant; but in their cross-examination it appeared that they boarded with the plaintiff, but neither of them had any lawful means of obtaining a livelihood. Judgment was rendered for the defendant, and the parties left the court-room. The plaintiff's attorney departed, grinning like a striped hyena, muttering curses not loud, but deep."

"The counsel for the defendant must have bribed the first witness in the case," quoth Uncle Zeb.

"There is where you are mistaken," I replied; "he neither gave nor promised her a single penny."

"What, then," asked my uncle, "was the cause of this sudden change in the witness?"

"Sir, I will explain it to you. Both the plaintiff and witnesses were disreputable females. The lawyer for the defendant obtained an interview with the plaintiff's principal witness, and he gave her the consoling information that if the case went against his client, he should feel under the necessity of entering complaints against the witnesses, for prostitution and night-walking, and have them sent to the House of Correction for six months; but if his client was discharged, it would place matters in a very different position. Do you see now why the witness turned so complete a somerset?"

The old gentleman laughed heartily, and remarked:

"Satan himself could not have invented a trick like that!"

"It is an incontrovertible fact," I continued, "that there are large numbers in the profession, who maintain a respectable standing, who are not a whit more honest than the pettifoggers. This class swindle on a larger scale. For example:—

"A few years ago, an American citizen had some dealings with a Spanish gentleman, who was a resident of 'Havana.' Some difficulty arose between them, respecting a certain contract. The American sued the Spaniard, who, wishing to return home, left in the hands of his attorney a sum sufficient to prosecute the case, or to settle the same amicably, if possible, without going into court. The American heard nothing of the matter, until the very day the case was to be brought up for trial, when he received a note from his attorney, informing him of the fact.

"'Why did you not give me earlier information of this?' he asked.

"'Because I did not suppose that you intended to have the case tried. I am certain you would lose it, if brought to trial, and the costs, which will amount to about ninety dollars, will be thrown upon you. If it was my case, I should let the matter drop where it stands, and thus save costs and expenses,' was the consoling reply of this lawyer.

"'Let me see the contract and documents,' said the client.

"The papers were handed to him, and he started directly for the Court House, remarking to the lawyer, as he passed out, 'If I should ever need your services again, I will let you know.' He sent in haste for his witnesses, went into court, managed his own case, and obtained the full amount of damages claimed.

"Thus you see that the maxim, 'A man who is his own lawyer, has a fool for his client,' does not always hold good. The two attornies, who had agreed to divide the spoils between them, were perfectly thunder-struck, when they found they were obliged to disgorge."

"Uncle Zeb" remarked: "But notwithstanding all this, you acknowledge that there are some upright lawyers, who deal with their clients honestly?"

"Certainly I do," was the reply; "but there are many upright and conscientious men, who, after they have been a short time in the profession, deviate from the path of rectitude, and in a few years it is almost impossible to tell what manner of men they are. The very atmosphere they breathe is polluted, and but few escape the infection. I have in my mind's eye, even now, an attorney, who commenced his studies in a light-house. He was 'poor but honest.' He managed to get through college, (Heaven only knows how,) and commenced the practise of law. His probity and attention to business soon gained for him many clients; but as soon as he obtained a position among his legal brethren, and in the community, he became an altered man, and can at the present time out-Herod Herod, in the tricks of the profession. He has not been known to speak the truth but once for several years. So says his partner, but I will not vouch for the truth of this statement.

"Turn from the 'Bar' to the 'Bench,'' and you will find those who were the honest and upright lawyers of their day. This remark is only applicable to Massachusetts. In those States where brawling, political partisans are elected to wear the robes of office, you cannot expect that the scales of justice will be held by honest hands. I have never heard of a single case where a Massachusetts Judge soiled the ermine, although there has been a few appointments which were not fit to be made.

"A venal Judge is a curse to any community, and I fear there are too many of them in the United States, as well as in other parts of the world. I once heard a well known Judge, after summing up the testimony in a case, remark: 'I must administer the law, as I find it upon the statute book, however obnoxious that law may be to me.' It is not every Judge who follows the example of this upright functionary."

CHAPTER IV.

Boston Police Department—Views of what a Police Officer should be—A singular but not uncommon case—An Officer falsifying his oath—Fernando Wood, Mayor of New York—The New York City Tombs—How Cases are there managed—Straw Bail—Difference between a New York Court Recorder, and a Boston Police Justice—The Goddess Justice is represented blindfolded; if Blind, she is not always Deaf—Shylock and the Farmer—Advice of Eminent Jurists, &c., &c.

BOSTON can boast of a better regulated Police Department than any other city in the Union. It consists of nearly three hundred members, including court officers, &c. The police officers proper, number two hundred and forty-six, who are distributed among eight stations. At each station there is a Captain and Lieutenant, while the whole department is under the direction and control of a Chief. He has no power, however, to appoint or discharge an officer. This prerogative is delegated to the Mayor of the city.

A police officer is an important personage, and is often placed in circumstances, where, if he does not use his discretionary powers aright, may do much serious injury to individuals and families. He should be a quiet, law-abiding man, himself, before he is entrusted with power whereby he can invoke the action of the law upon others, and so conduct himself in his official capacity, as to gain the confidence and respect of all good citizens with whom he may come in contact. He should not be an irascible or vindictive man, but cool, deliberate and determined. There are many attached to the police department of Boston, and other cities, whose places might be supplied with better men. For the past few years, the fitness of the candidate who applies for the badge of a policeman, has been estimated by his political opinions; a man who has not worked well for the party in power, stands but a poor chance, however worthy and capable he may be. A careful observer, who visits the criminal courts in the city of Boston, will discover that it is not always the best and most efficient officers who make the most arrests, and enter the most complaints. Some officers, who are stationed in the worst sections in the city, will not enter as many complaints as others who are stationed, in more quiet parts of the metropolis. Some officers will enter a house where there is rioting and disturbance, and in a few moments all will be peace and quietude. Others might go in among the same party, and under the same circumstances, and a general melee would ensue. The next day, some four or five persons would be arraigned before the court, charged with disturbing the peace, and assaulting the police officers, while in the discharge of their duty. A police officer should be a temperate man, and if he uses alcoholic drinks at all, it should be with great moderation. It is not three years ago, since I saw a police officer go into court, to enter a complaint against a man for drunkenness, who was himself so intoxicated that he could not sign his name to the requisite document. His services, however, were not required after that day.

It sometimes happens that a police officer will enter complaints against citizens for the violation of some city ordinance, such as smoking in the street, neglecting to remove snow from their sidewalks, &c., when a simple notification, or a few words with the party at fault, would have been far better than a prosecution.

One of these kind of cases was brought before Judge Rogers, not long since. The defendant was complained of for not removing the snow from the sidewalk in front of his dwelling, numbered 46 B—— St., within twenty-four hours after the snow had fallen. The defendant plead "not guilty," and requested the postponement of the case, to enable him to bring witnesses for the defence.

"I should have supposed you would come prepared to defend your case," said the Judge.

"So I should, your Honor," replied the wag, "if I had only known what the complaint was. At first I thought it was for thrashing a 'negro ostler;' but I went and paid him seven and sixpence, and he acknowledged satisfaction. Then I didn't know but what it was for keeping a big bull-dog, called "Roaring Jake," unlicensed, and I brought a witness here to prove that I sold out all my right, title and interest in him, more than a year ago; but I did not come prepared to defend the sidewalk case."

"What do you expect to prove by your witnesses, if the case is postponed?" asked the Judge.

"Several things," was the reply. "In the first place, I intend to show that there are but twelve houses on the street, consequently there could be no number 46; also, to show that this street is not a public highway, and, furthermore, to show that I never lived in any house on that street, and what is more, I never intend to!"

The defendant had an acquaintance among the spectators, who was called to the witness stand. He testified that the defendant had boarded with him for the last three months in another section of the city, that the defendant visited the house spoken of in the complaint, three or four times a week, for the purpose of giving music lessons, and that the occupant of the house and the defendant were both of the same name.

It is needless to add that *this* case was indefinitely postponed.

Errors like this are unpardonable in police officers, and although they may sometimes amuse a crowd of idle spectators, they take up the time of the court, are an expense to the State, and very annoying to the prosecuted parties.

Some police officers are very "swift witnesses," when they are on the witness-stand. I recollect a case where a middle aged man, tolerably well dressed, was brought up for assaulting a gentleman in the street, the night previous. The officer testified that he saw the assault committed, and thought it was of an aggravated nature. While he was upon the stand, the assaulted party came into court. He also was called up to the stand, and testified that the prisoner jostled him off the sidewalk, and used some abusive language, but did not injure him at all, neither did he put him in any bodily fear.

After the trial was concluded, I heard the gentleman say that the policeman did not see the assault, but that he himself met the police officer, subsequently, and stated the circumstance, walked back with him to the place where the prisoner was standing, and pointed out the man.

I do not pretend to say that such cases often occur; but I do say that a police officer who will, upon the witness-stand, "go it blind," (to use a sporting phrase,) is not a fit man for the office.

What a mighty change has taken place in the police departments in the cities of New York and Boston, within the past seven years! The time was when there were men employed to protect the citizens in their property, who were not much better than highwaymen and pickpockets! The stool-pigeon system was carried out to an alarming extent. No man, who had been once convicted of a crime, however sincere his reformation might have been, was secure against the machinations of those "devils incarnate," who were at that time placed in those offices of power and trust.

In another chapter I shall explain at length the *modus operandi* of those police officers who carried out the stool-pigeon system to its fullest extent in the principal cities of the Union.

Fernando Wood, the present efficient Mayor of New York, has done more to reform abuses in the police department of that city, than any other man who has occupied the Mayor's chair for the last twenty years. Under his administration, policemen do not venture to lounge in grog-shops and bar-rooms. Too many of them have received their walking-tickets, and when they applied to him, and inquired what complaints were preferred against them, they found that his Honor himself was the complainant; that he had watched them at times when they least expected it, and found them remiss in their duties. Happy would it be, for both citizens and policemen, if the Mayors of all our cities would follow the example of this indefatigable man.

I have not so much experience with the arrangements

of the Recorder's office in the "New York Tombs," as I have in the Police Court Room of Boston, but things are managed there somewhat differently. We will look in for a few moments, and examine it.

Here we find (when there are a large number of cases awaiting examination,) it is all bustle and confusion. Officers, rushing around, looking for their witnesses — lawyers, picking up their victims among the prisoners — spectators, jabbering in every language known since the builders of the Tower of Babel refused to work, because they could not understand each other's dialect.

Here witnesses are allowed to tell their own story, in their own way, without interruption from Recorder or officers. I will sketch the following examination of a stage-struck cyprian, as an illustration :

A young woman was introduced to the Recorder, who gloried in the *sobriquet* of Sophronia Fitzclarence, who had been arrested at the instance of a cabman. She was brought in with hair dishevelled, bonnet knocked into a "cocked hat," and her dress in disorder.

The cab-driver—who was a sinister looking chap, with an oblique cast in his eye, a very large head, and an enormously stout neck—was the principal witness against Sophronia, and appeared to be as much of a character as the accused herself.

"Well sir," said the Recorder, "what did Sophronia do to you?"

"Vell, if you'll jest hold your hosses a minute or two, I'll give you all the items," retorted the cabman, with the peculiar *patois* of his class.

"Go on, then," continued the Recorder.

"Yes, sir; vell, as I was standing 'side my cab, sir, near the corner of St. Charles and Poydras streets, a thinkin' on several things, but nothin' in particular, except my fares, 'cause you see it had been a dull day, this here critter come stormin' along, with a kind of theatre step, and jest as she got up to me, she stop't suddently, give me a wild stare in the face, slapped her hands together, worked her shoulders backward, and then kinder shrieked out:

'Oh! Clifford! is that you?'

'No, I'm d—d if it is,' said I.

"But afore the words was scarcely out of my mouth, she threw back both her arms, and rushed up, grabbing me round the neck, jest as if it was her own dearest blood relation; then she pushed me off at arm's length, looked me full in the eye; says she:

'Clifford, don't you know me?'

'Vell I don't,' says I.

'Speak to me, Clifford,' says she.

'Go away,' says I.

'My own Clifford,' says she.

'You be d—d,' says I.

"And then she sobbed, threw her hands about in a

sort of distraction kind of way, and screamed out agin:

'Clifford, vy vont you speak to me?'

'Cos I don't know you,' says I.

'There, that's Clifford's voice, if ever Clifford spoak,' says she.

'I'm d—d if it was,' says I; 'my name is Jem Thomas, and I don't know your Clifford from a side of sole leather.'

"Vell, she went on in jest that way, swingin' her arms round, spoutin' poetry, and talkin' nonsense, jest like as if she was a play-actor on the stage, till after a spell I had to call a watchman, to help me out of the scrape. Oh! she's one of the dreadfulest critters of the highstrikes breed I ever did see. Vy, do you know, your Honor, she axed me if her 'orrid nupshals could be perwented?"

"I didn't know it," gravely replied the Recorder. "But what did you say to her?"

"Vell, your Honor, I said as how I thought if she'd go home, and take a drop, it might perwent 'em, although I didn't know what them nupshals she was making such a muss about was. Don't you think that sleep 'ud hit her case?"

"Very likely," replied the Recorder.

"And, vot's more, don't you think if she was to take the temperance pledge, it wouldn't hurt her much?" continued the cabman, giving the Recorder a knowing wink.

"That will do," replied his Honor ; and Jem was allowed to depart.

Miss Sophronia confessed she had been to the theatre, and imbibed a quantity of stimulating drinks. These, combined with a great fondness and a natural taste for the drama, had turned her brain for the moment ; but she promised to behave better for the future, if the Recorder would only let her off. She was discharged.

In the criminal courts of New York, thieves, burglars, incendiaries, and criminals of the like class, often escape punishment, from the fact that the Judges, from some cause known only to themselves, will often take what is called "straw bail," for the appearance of the prisoners at the higher court.

In that city, a man can, or I should say could, at one time, go before a magistrate, and swear that he is worth ten thousand dollars, when in reality he is not worth a thousand cents. When the case comes up for trial, neither prisoner or bondsman can be found ; or if the bondsman is found, and it is conclusively shown that he is not, nor never was worth one hundred dollars, is he indicted for perjury ? No ! we find but few cases upon record. The prisoner escapes, and the bondsman or accomplice goes free. But this is New York justice as it has been administered in the Empire City.

In Massachusetts, the courts are differently managed. It is not often that "straw bail" is taken ; and if persons offering themselves, are accepted as bondsmen in a criminal case, do not produce the prisoner on the day of trial, or stand ready to "fork over" the full amount of the defaulted bonds, woe betide them.

A curious illustration of this fact occurred in the Police Court of Boston, a short time since. A gentleman was arraigned for violation of the liquor law, and convicted. He appealed to a higher court. He was required to give good and sufficient sureties, in the sum of two hundred dollars, for his appearance to prosecute the same. A well known individual, who is worth two hundred thousand dollars, offered himself as bondsman. The Judge asked the usual question:

"Do you own real estate?"

"I do," was the reply.

"To what amount?" asked the Judge.

"I do not see fit to communicate my own private affairs, neither will I tell what I consider my property worth," was the answer.

The Judge refused to take the gentleman for bondsman, and the defendant was obliged to procure another, who willingly stated that he was not worth more than seven hundred dollars, free and clear of all liabilities.

This occurrence caused much merriment at the time, among the friends and acquaintances of the wealthy man, and in consequence of it many jokes have been perpetrated at his expense.

This conclusively shows how tenaciously some of the old Justices and Judges of Massachusetts will cling to the puritanical forms of a past age. If in the case I have just related, the gentleman who offered himself as bondsman had been a stranger in the city, the course pursued by the Judge would have been justifiable and proper; but in a case where Judge, clerks, officers, and perhaps almost every person in the Court House, knew the estimated wealth of the man, the action of the Judge appeared absurd and ridiculous.

Justice, as administered in our courts of law, is not always blind. True, the Goddess is represented in prints and statues with her eyes closely bandaged, holding in her hand even balanced scales. But is there any one so demented as to suppose for a moment that the blind Goddess is without feeling. Is she deaf, as well as blind? When a bag of shining gold is thrown in one scale, and a farthing into the other, is it reasonable to suppose that she is so egregriously stupid that she cannot tell the difference? Judges and jurors are but mortal men; hold a gold eagle before your own eye, and can you see through it? Certainly not. How then can you expect others, whose optical powers are no greater than your own, to do so? He must be a self-sacrificing man indeed, and differently constituted from his fellow-men, who can dash the yellow scales to the earth, and look upon guilt with a single eye, when its robes glitter with diamonds. How true were the words of the celebrated "John Randolph:" "Wealth and power will unite; they will come together as naturally as the sexes."

Let us look into the court-room, and see if this is correct. Look at that man on yonder seat. He appears, nervous, anxious, and ill at ease. His father died a few years ago, and left him a splendid farm, free from all incumbrance. A Shylock, with whom he became acquainted, advised him to go into some speculation, and offered to advance him such sums of money as he might require, Shylock taking a mortgage on the farm. The poor fellow took his advice, and here he is, without a dollar in his pocket, while Shylock has obtained possession of all his property, for about one-quarter part of its actual value. The poor man has worked early and late to earn a sufficient sum of money to bring his case before the court, and show that the transfer of the property was a fraudulent transaction, which it certainly was, beyond the possibility of doubt. His legal adviser is a young man, unnoticed, and almost unknown, but he must employ him, for want of means to fee an abler and a better man.

But here comes Shylock, attended by his counsellors. He has secured the best legal talent that could be obtained in the State. He has with him, in the court, some half a dozen creatures of his own, who are ready to swear to almost anything their master requires. His attornies complacently re-examined the deeds and documents which the hoary headed sinner, their client, had obtained by deception, misrepresentation and fraud, from one weak in intellect, and easily imposed upon.

Poor devil! you'll get plenty of law here, but I fear, no justice. The trial proceeds—the lawyers argue—the Judge charges the Jury—a verdict for the defendant is rendered—Shylock has established his rights to the property—and poor Pillocoddy leaves the court-room, undetermined in his own mind, whether he had better go and hang himself, or ship on board a whaler.

Let me not be misunderstood. Let no one imagine that I would imply, in the case stated, or in any other case I may allude to, that the Judge and Jury did not decide strictly according to the law and evidence, as they had sworn upon their oaths to do. But this I do say, that the poor man cannot cope with his more wealthy neighbor, in our courts of law.

It sometimes hpppens that a poor man will have a case where law, evidence, and everything else, is in his favor, but he cannot raise money enough to carry on his suit, and is obliged to apply to some friend or acquaintance, who is in better circumstances than himself, and will agree to give him one-half of the amount claimed, if his case is successful, provided he will advance the required sums necessary to prosecute his claims.

We will suppose that after long litigation, and months,

perhaps years of vexation and trouble, a man is successful, and he obtains a verdict in his favor. His friend takes one-half of the sum, and after he has paid all the contingent expenses, the man is but little, perhaps no better off than when he commenced the suit. The law's delay has often caused many a worthy man to become sick at heart, and has brought many to a premature grave. A noted Judge was once asked the question, what course he would pursue, if a man of means and ability owed him twenty pounds, and refused to pay. The Judge replied, "rather than commence an action at law against him, I would give the rascal ten pounds more, and then cancel the debt." Another Judge, equally famous in his day, while giving advice to his son, who was about to commence business in the world for himself, cautioned him to avoid all litigation. "If," said he, "a man should claim the coat upon your back, and assure you that unless you delivered it up, he would commence a suit at law for its recovery, strip it off, and give it to him, lest that in defending the coat, you may lose your hat and breeches also."

The most casual observer will notice that those men who have the most knowledge of the laws, but seldom enter into litigation themselves; it is those who know the least of them, who are entrapped in the meshes.

CHAPTER V.

The Stool-Pigeon business as it has been carried out in Boston, New-York, and other cities in the United States—The *modus operandi* of Police Officers who use Convicts for Stool-Pigeons—An infernal practice—Testimony of a State Official—The Gamblers—Their supposed connection with the Police Department—Plans concocted to induce men to visit Gaming Hells—The Descent made upon the Gambling Houses in Boston, in the year 1851—Grand Exhibition of Gamblers' Tools aud Implements, in the City Hall—How those Gambling Implements were afterwards disposed of—Confession of a Noted Gambler—Licensed Brothels and Gaming Houses.

IN the preceding chapter, I spoke of the stool-pigeon system, as it was extensively carried on in Boston, New York, and other cities in the States. As there are but few persons who fully understand the operations of this most outrageous scheme, concocted for the express purpose of leading men to commit crime, and then entrapping them, I will endeavor to throw some light upon the subject.

The police officers who are connected with the thief-catching department in the different cities, generally know when the term of service of each convict who has been sent to the State Prison for burglary, robbery, &c.,

HINMAN MEREDITH.

(See Page 285.)

expires. The officers in New York, Philadelphia, and other cities, are informed when convicts are to be discharged from Charlestown prison; while the officers in Boston know equally well when convicts are to be set at liberty from Sing-Sing, Auburn, and other prisons.

When prisoners are discharged, they do not usually remain long in the vicinity, or State, where they were convicted; but no sooner do they arrive in another city, (and oftentimes the telegraph announces their departure from the place where they were last seen,) when the thief-catchers are on the alert to "spot" them, and watch all their movements. A well tried and trusty officer of the thief catching stamp will manage to fall in with one of the most reckless and hardened of the convicts; he will inquire how long he has been liberated? What business he intends to follow? Whether he has any money to support him until he can obtain work? Then, after expressing the most kindly feelings, (if the convict is out of funds, which of course they generally are,) he will give him a few dollars, and appoint a time and place to meet him again.

At the time appointed, the officer and convict will meet, and the latter will receive his instructions from the former. The officer will inform the convict that there is in the city another recently discharged convict, and he has every reason to believe that the rascal intends to return to his old business—house-breaking.

The officer will then inform the convict where his victim is located, and tell him, he must ferret him out—scrape an acquaintance, if he does not already know him—inform him that he also is a brother convict—"sound him from the lowest note, to the top of his compass," and discover, if possible, what course he intends to pursue in future. The officer promises the convict that he shall be well paid for any discoveries which he may make, and pledges him his word of honor that whatever may be done between them, he (the convict stool-pigeon,) shall be protected, and unmolested.

Let us now follow the stool-pigeon. He falls in with his brother in crime, and as they set conversing together, in some obscure bar-room, imbibing that enemy, which, when put into a man's mouth, will "steal away his brains," you could overhear the following conversation:—

Stool-pigeon. "Well, Jem, what's best for us to do?

Jem. "I've about made up my mind to get a situation, go to work at my trade, and try to gain a position in society; 'cause you see that our old business won't pay."

Stool-pigeon. "That's my mind, exactly. Long enough afore I served out my last term at Sing-Sing, says I to myself, 'taint no use for a man to spend all the days of his life in working for the State, and living on rotten beef: now if I could only get a good chance to work at my trade, I would try and be honest for a little spell, anyhow. I believe I'm about as good a blacksmith as can be found round these diggings."

Jem. "As a cabinet-maker, I won't turn my back to any man. This morning I saw an advertisement in the newspaper, of a place where cabinet-makers were wanted. I went up, and applied for a situation; the 'old man asked me where I worked last? I told him that I worked for my father, in Manchester, N. H. The 'old cuss' looked at me as though he thought I was lying, but he told me to come to-morrow, at twelve o'clock, and he would give me an answer. Now if I only get a chance there, I shall be a man among the rest; 'cause you see they won't have any means of finding out that I was ever a prison-bird."

Stool-pigeon. "Good, old boy! I wish I had so good a show before me; but let's take another drink, just to drive away the blue-devils. I hope you will be successful. I've got a chance in view, but if I don't get the situation, I don't know which way to turn next. By the bye, my old boy, do you know any of our old 'pals,' who are circulating round the city now?"

Jem. "Only one; that's Seth Brummell—he's got a 'sit' in the H—— Theatre; gets a 'sal' of six dollars a week, as stage door-keeper. But between you and me, his 'sit' is worth more than five times that amount to him."

Stool-pigeon. "How's that?"

Jem. "'Cause you see he gets the halves and quarters out of those fellows who want to get in behind the scenes ; he slides 'em in, and so you see he makes a good thing on't — some of the actors have missed things from their dressing-rooms ; nobody suspects 'Seth,' — some poor 'ballet girl,' or supernumary, is charged with the larceny."

Stool-pigeon. "Well, Jem, let's retire now ; and I will meet you here to-morrow night, at eight o'clock, and we will talk matters over. For my part, I'm 'hard up ;' and if I don't get a chance to go to work 'pooty' soon, I shan't have funds enough to pay for a night's lodging."

Jem. "Same here ; but by J—s, if I don't get that place, to-morrow, I don't know what I shall do."

Stool-pigeon. "Keep up good pluck, my old fellow, boys of our kind ain't easily discouraged ; and recollect we are now sworn friends, and we will meet again to-morrow night."

The convicts shake hands, and part.

Let us now follow the stool-pigeon, and we shall find him in secret confab with the officer. That functionary will be fully advised of all that has passed between the convicts. By some hocus-pocus arrangement, the employer, on whom convict number two was to call, with the expectancy of obtaining work, becomes aware of the fact that his applicant has just graduated from State Prison, and of course he will not employ him. He leaves the counting-room, disappointed and dejected, not knowing what move to make next; and when

"Night throws her sable mantle o'er the earth,"

he seeks the company of his friend, the stool-pigeon.

They meet, and we will again listen to their conversation:—

Stool-pigeon. "Well, my old hearty, what news today? Did you get the chance to work at your trade you spoke of last night?"

Jem. "Curses on my luck! No! I went at the appointed time, and the old fellow looked at me as though he thought I came for the express purpose of cutting his throat. I'm satisfied well enough, that some devil has 'spotted' me, and the old man has found out who I am."

Stool-pigeon. "That's exactly my case. I've been disappointed in the same way, myself, to-day. When I went to see the man who as good as promised to give me employment, the hypocritical old fool grinned like an enraged monkey; and says he: 'My friend, I should be glad to give you employment, but I don't like your antecedents; I don't like your proclivities!' So you see I'm 'spotted,' too, and I am almost out of funds; but as long as there's a shot left in the locker, I'll go snacks with you."

Jem. "Thank you, my dear fellow; but the fact is, I don't know what to do, or which way to turn."

Stool-pigeon. "I've been thinking, if I could only make a raise, I'd start for Australia, mighty quick; you wouldn't find me long round in these 'diggins.'"

Jem. "Jist give me an opportunity, and I'll do the same thing."

Stool-pigeon. "Well, it's no use to try and get employment, or raise a dollar in any way the world calls honest. I'd rather be back in my old quarters, the prison, than to be hunted down like a wild beast, without sufficient money in my pocket to support me."

Jem. "So had I. I will not starve; and if I can't earn money, I must get it some other way. You're a single man, but I've a wife and children, I dearly love."

Stool-pigeon. "No! But are you foolish enough to suppose that she thinks of you now? Who ever heard of a woman remaining true to a man for five years after he has been caged? Ha! ha! ha!"

Jem. "In that you're mistaken. The prison-chaplain has often seen my wife, and he tells me that she has supported herself and her little boy by her industry, and was looking anxiously forward to the day of my liberation."

Stool-pigeon. "A wonderful woman, truly! Have you seen her, yet?"

Jem. "No. I thought I would get a chance to go

to work, get me a new suit of clothes, have a few dollars in my pocket, then return to her. O! I've looked forward to that happy hour; but I find all my hopes blasted, and I care not how soon the prison-gates again close upon me, and shut me out forever from the world."

Stool-pigeon. "Pooh! pooh! pooh! Don't be down-hearted, comrade; there is a good time coming."

Jem. "When? When? How? Six years ago I was a contented and a happy man. I served my apprenticeship at my trade, and remained with my employer, he giving me the highest wages paid to journeymen. I formed an appetite for intoxicating drinks; I neglected my business; my wife, who was a meek and gentle spirit, remonstrated with me, but in vain; I abused her; I went on, step by step, and at last fell into the company of a notorious house-breaker. Being destitute of money, and driven to desperation, I reluctantly agreed to assist him in a robbery, which was successful, and we obtained about fifteen dollars. He escaped, how, I know not. I was taken, tried, and convicted. O God! that I were dead!"

Stool-pigeon. "Well, my boy, you must keep up pluck. My case is pretty much the same as yours, only I hain't got 'no wife. Now suppose we should see a good chance? Hush! there's no one listening, is there? I say, suppose that we could see a good chance to relieve some rich old curmudgeon of a small amount of his ill-gotten wealth, with no chance of detection, will you join me ?"

Jem. "No! I'll rob no more."

Stool-pigeon. "What! not if you can raise money enough to leave this cursed place, and get to the gold mines, with a small sum to leave your wife and boy until your return ? Then you know you might repay all you had taken, and have a pocket full of rocks left. How is that, eh ?"

Jem. "What is it you would propose ?"

Stool-pigeon. "In the plan I have in view it will be impossible to get along without a third man. I have my eye on a jeweller's store in W—— St., which can be entered mighty easy. No watchman, no bull-dog about the premises ; there we can make a glorious raise, and if you have a mind to join me, say the word, and the fur flies."

Jem. "I don't know what to do; but if you think it's a safe operation"—

Stool-pigeon. "Safe! I never saw so safe a chance in my life; there can't be any mistake about it."

Jem. "But who are we to get for a third 'pal.' "

Stool-pigeon. "How's your friend, Seth Brummell ? Go and sound him ; I'll wait here till you return."

The victim starts, and after a short delay, returns with the pleasing information that "Seth" is ready to go into the arrangement, if there is a fair show.

Stool-pigeon. "Tell him to meet us here to-morrow night. Now we'll take a parting glass, then I'll go up and twig round the premises; you'd better not go with me, 'cause it wouldn't be well for us to be seen together. There's nothing like being on the safe side, you know."

The worthy couple separate; one goes to his lodgings, the other to inform his employer, (the stool-pigeon officer,) of his success.

Shortly afterwards, an extensive robbery is committed, and announced in the papers of the day as one of the most daring and successful burglaries on record. The public are informed that although our active and efficient police are on the *qui vive*, no trace had been discovered of the goods or the robbers. Advertisements and handbills are extensively circulated, offering a reward of five hundred or a thousand dollars for the recovery of the goods, and arrest of the robbers. After a reasonable time has elapsed, you will read in the public journals of the day, an announcement like this:

STOLEN PROPERTY RECOVERED!!

ARREST OF TWO OF THE BURGLARS!!!

"It gives us great pleasure to inform the public that, through the indefatigable exertions of those worthy and efficient officers, Messrs. 'Grab-'um-quick' and 'Catch-'um-easy,' a large portion of the goods taken by the robbers from the store of Messrs. C—— and T——, on the night of the 20th inst., have been recovered. They were found in an old barn, on the S—— turnpike, and two of the burglars have been arrested. Both of them are old prison-birds; one goes by the name of James ——, the other, Seth Brummell. It is supposed they had an accomplice, who escaped. These desperadoes will now have an opportunity to serve the State a few years longer, where they can neither rob nor molest honest citizens."

While these two men, (these stool-pigeon dupes,) are brought up, tried, convicted, and sent over, where is the stool-pigeon? I must answer, as old deacon Foster usually does, when he is in doubt: "raly, I don-no, but I guess he is somewhere round." I will not pretend to say that he "fobs" any portion of the reward paid over to the officers, but I have a right to think aloud, as the countryman did, when he was intently gazing at a string of huge sausages, and remarked, *sotto voce:* "Where they make that kind 'er sarsengers, you'll find the dogs wery scarce."

But in all honesty I would ask, why is it that the prime movers, directors, and those who are the very head and front of the offending, in almost every case where an extensive robbery has been committed, have been suffered to escape, while the unfortunate dupes and tools of their machinations, are arrested, tried, convicted and punished. I grant that "one murder makes a villain, millions a hero," but I have yet to learn that notorious robbers and scoundrels can benefit mankind by being suffered to run at large, inveigling men more honest than themselves, and inciting them to commit crimes which are sure to bring them to a felon's cell.

Perhaps the reader will ask, can it be possible that such scenes as you have represented have ever transpired in Massachusetts?

I answer, yes! Aye, and more than this! There have been scenes enacted in the city of Boston, of a similar kind, which might well shame "Old Cerberus," and cause him to deliver up his keys, when one of these minions approached his gate.

In a previous chapter I spoke of Fernando Wood. That man, as I before remarked, did much to rectify the many abuses which had from time to time crept into the New York police department. Benjamin Seaver did the same in the Boston police department. When he came into office, he found the department rotten to the very core. He could not understand how it was that policemen and other officers happened to be endowed with that astute knowledge which would lead them into gardens and garrets, and discover stolen property; being a skeptic in the science of clairvoyance, he examined for himself, and suddenly there was a great change. He said to the Aldermen, "I take the responsibility to change and alter the police department, but I cannot, nor will not, tell you the why's and wherefore's." He did change—he did alter—without bringing any charges against the guilty parties. He looked after the police department personally, and if he made a few mistakes in the appointment of officers afterwards, it was the fault of the head, and not of the heart. One thing is certain; he broke up for the time the stool-pigeon business in the city of Boston, and I do not believe that it can again be revived.

Is it not a lamentable fact, that a scheme so revolting, and so repugnant to the better feelings of man, should ever have been put in operation, and carried out, in the puritanical city of Boston? Methinks I hear the reader say, this system may have been practiced in other cities, but I cannot believe that it was ever introduced into Boston!

Notwithstanding your disbelief, kind reader, I can assure you that the stool-pigeon system has been practised to a greater extent, in years past, in the city of Boston, than in any other city in the United States!

In verification of this assertion, I have the testimony of a worthy and much esteemed State officer, who had an opportunity to thoroughly investigate such matters. He, I doubt not, knew more of this system, and the kindred iniquities which were its concomitants, than he ever rehearsed or wrote. Yea, in the city which is noted throughout the continent for its excellent schools, its multiplicity of churches, its charitable associations and institutions, there are deeds of darkness committed, by men holding high offices, which are never brought to light. At least, such has been the case in years past.

There are but few thief-catchers and thief-detecters who are initiated into the mysteries of the stool-pigeon system. Their brother officers are as ignorant of their proceedings as the community at large. When a large robbery is committed, there is generally a large reward offered for the recovery of the property. Every police officer is at once on the look-out. They want, if possible, to discover the valuables, arrest the robber or robbers, claim the reward, and obtain that meed of praise from the community, for their efficiency and success, which is always sure to follow.

But it is the stool-pigeon officer who discovers the property, arrests the thieves, and receives the reward.

True, it is sometimes incomprehensible, to officers and others, when a stool-pigeon officer makes a discovery of the kind alluded to, how it is that their perceptive faculties, and sharp-sightedness, so far exceeds those of other men, who possess an equal, if not a larger amount of brains than themselves. How is it, they say, that they can go to the exact spot, and find stolen property, that has been buried in the earth? How came they possessed of this magic wand, which will lead them directly to those places, which appear to be unknown to all others except themselves? Go and clip the wings of the stool-pigeon, and he will answer these questions.

Heaven be praised! this cursed system is not practised to any great extent, at the present time, in any of our principal cities, and I do not believe that scarcely a vestige of it remains in the city of Boston; or if there is, it is conducted on a remarkably small scale.

The chief operators have been discharged from office, and many of them have left this section of the country, for new fields of enterprise, in a more congenial clime.

I will now devote a small space to the gambling fraternity, and their relation with the police department, in the different cities of the Union.

By some it has been said, (and perhaps there may be some truth in their assertions,) that police officers are well paid, by the proprietors of gaming saloons, who fee the officers to protect them, or what is synonymous, pass them without molestation. For a certain stipend, it is said, the officer agrees to dispense with his eyes and ears, whenever he is in or about their premises. He agrees to see nothing, hear nothing, save and except in a case where some poor unfortunate, who had been swindled out of his money, should attempt to make a disturbance, by demanding a certain portion of it back, or at least, a sufficient sum to pay his board-bill, and a passage to his own home. In such cases the sporting gentleman expect and demand that the officer shall take the victim to the watch or station-house, and then get rid of him as quietly as possible.

If the swindled victim should have the audacity to enter a complaint before a magistrate, the police officer is expected to swear that the man went into the gentlemen's club-room, and being intoxicated, he caused so great a disturbance that they were obliged to eject him from the premises.

This may be all true, when applied to officers in some cities, but few cases of the kind have ever come to light in the city of Boston. We must therefore, necessarily conclude, that either the sporting gentlemen, or the police officers, (perhaps both,) are more honest here than they are in other cities.

Never having been a gambler myself, and never having visited a gaming saloon more than three or four times in my life, and then from curiosity, going in as a spectator, it cannot be expected that I can be well informed, by personal experience or observation, of all the tricks, plans, devices and traps which are made and laid to ensnare the unwary, and so fascinate them that they will almost involuntarily enter these "gates of Hell."

From what little knowledge I have of gaming operations, in this and other countries, I am convinced, when that passion is once established, it will over-balance and overpower every other passion of the human heart. It is cherished and followed by all classes and conditions of men. The hatless and shoeless newsboy, who hawks his papers about the street, can be found after his morning's labor, in some by-lane, or obscure place, pitching his coppers with his associates, and will return at nightfall, penniless, to his widowed mother, who is dependant on his earnings for the means to procure a supper for herself and her younger children. The apprentice, who for some extra work receives a dollar, will resort to some low bar-room, where he finds those older than himself, engaged in "raffling" for a worthless watch, or some other useless trinket. He also returns home penniless, and as he retires to his bed, looks at his worn-out shoes, and regrets that he did not use his money in purchasing a new pair. He forswears visiting the saloon again, but when he receives another dollar, you will find him revisiting the same place, determined to win back the money he has already lost.

The mechanic who has toiled early and late, during the week, and receives his hard earned wages on Saturday night, says to himself, I must have a little recreation, and before I purchase my provisions for the coming week, I will step into the —— Saloon, and take a drop of brandy and water. He there finds acquaintances, some of whom he considers his friends. He has fifteen dollars in his pocket, and as he feels rich, he invites them all to drink at his expense. The crowd accepts his invitation, (men who congregate in bar-rooms seldom refuse such invitations,) and our mechanic finds one dollar of his wages transferred from his pocket to the till of the bar-keeper. Another and another of his brother mechanics propose to repeat the dose, as they do not wish to be considered mean.

When the whole party become somewhat excited with copious draughts of adulterated liquor, the gentlemanly proprietor will invite the crowd into an adjoining room, assuring them that in a very short time a splendid lunch would be served up, and he could not consent to have his company leave without partaking thereof, as it was especially fixed for them.

The mechanic goes in with the crowd—Props are introduced—he loses his week's wages—he returns home to his family late at night, inebriated, and without a dollar in his pocket.

Then we have the clerk, who is perhaps one of the best book-keepers in the city of Boston. With much persuasion a fellow clerk prevails upon him to drop into a gaming saloon, (one of the most respectable class;) he wanted to look in, merely for amusement. The young clerk reluctantly enters, and looks upon the game with great interest. His friend pointing to the "Faro" table, says, "The king of hearts is the winning card, and I'm going to put a five spot on that, just for luck." He put the money down—he won—he then staked the ten dollars, and again he won. The young clerk, his companion, was much excited, and resolved to try his luck at the gaming-board. He tried—at first won—then lost—then stole from his employers—then was sent to State Prison!

We will now ascend one step higher in the gaming ladder, coming to the merchant. He visits no gaming saloons, not he! He deprecates all institutions of this kind, and calls upon our law-makers to enact penal statutes to suppress them. Nevertheless, if you watch him carefully, you will see that two or three times during the week, he will visit the club-room to which he belongs; and if an acquaintance or customer has been invited to "just drop in" and take a social glass, he is ready to play with him a game of "brag," or "euchre," for one, three, or five hundred dollars. This, of course, is not gambling, in his estimation; it is only pastime, to pass away a leisure hour.

Thus we see that the proclivities of all men, who do not steadily set their faces against it, and whose motto is, "Touch not, handle not," will imperceptibly become gamblers, while they themselves sincerely believe—and even after they are ruined, will conscientiously place their hands upon their breast, and say—although I have been unfortunate, thank God, I have never gambled!

When our merchant-princes erect magnificent buildings in every city in the Union, calling them club-rooms, while in reality they are, and should be called, gambling rooms for the "upper ten"—buildings and rooms that no police officer dare to enter, and where thousands of dollars nightly change hands. Why should laws be enacted that will consign the news-boy, the mechanic, or the clerk, to a felon's cell, while they have before their eyes an example set by those whom they are led to consider as their superiors and betters? I will freely admit that the game of "chance" has been known and played since the days of old father "Adam." He tasted the forbidden fruit, and if we believe what all distinguished theologians have taught us, every one of his sons and daughters are more or less inclined to follow the example set by their great progenitor.

The human mind craves excitement, and if it does not find it in one source, it will in another. The ever-changing, restless brain of man, will seek out new sources, and if it does not find gratification in one, it will speedily resort to another. There is nothing more fascinating ever yet discovered, than the game of "chance." Old Adam played, and lost, and his posterity will, as they ever have, follow his example, down to the end of time.

Within the past two or three years, many of the most prominent and extensive gaming establishments in New York have been broken up. Broken up, did I say? No! The proprietors have only changed their location; for when they are driven out of one place, they will immediately locate themselves in another. Their customers will soon become advised of the change, and follow them. In the city of Boston, the police department have not meddled with the gaming fraternity, to any great extent, for the last three or four years; and they had much better leave them unmolested in their profession, than to re-enact the scenes of the last great haul of gamblers, which took place in 1851.

At that time the whole police department were directed to make a simultaneous descent on every gaming saloon in the city of Boston, except the "upper ten." They were ordered to arrest every person found on the premises, and carry them to Jail. They were to seize all the implements used for gaming which they might find on the premises, and take them up to the City Hall, to be used as evidence against the accused.

On the following Monday, the accused parties were arraigned in the Police Court. All of them waived an examination; paid their fines of three dollars and costs each, and were suffered to depart.

Great was the excitement among the saints and sinners of the metropolis, when the announcement was made that there would be a public exhibition, in the City Hall, of all the gaming implements seized on that ever memorable, and never to be forgotten occasion.

From morn till eve, the vestibule of the building was crowded to excess. Old and young, high and low, pubicans and hypocrites, all rushed, in one heterogeneous mass, to gaze upon the trophies which had been seized in (what some of them pleased to term) devils' dens.

On long tables, guarded by officers, the gaming implements were carefully arranged. There were Faro-banks, dealing-boxes, for cards, counters, or checks, some of them inlaid with pearl and gold, Roulette tables, Dice-boxes, Props, Sweat-cloths, and many other articles used by the sporting fraternity.

The heroes of this wonderful feat were moving about among the spectators, listening with much complacency to the encomiums lavished upon them by some simpering boarding-school Miss, or antiquated damsel, who had passed "into the sear and yellow leaf."

After this grand exhibition was brought to a close, I looked for an announcement of the grand finale, viz. :—the burning and destruction of these contraband articles, by order of the Court, as provided and directed by law. But they were not destroyed, and I do not believe that one man out of a thousand in the community ever knew what became of them. "'Tis true, alas! and pity 'tis, 'tis true," that in less than six weeks after this grand exploit, many of the sporting gentlemen had, (for a consideration,) recovered their tools and apparatuses, most of which were very costly and valuable.

Strange to say, there was not a single man in the Board of Aldermen, who had sufficient moral courage to introduce an order, demanding the appointment of a committee to investigate, and report in the matter. It would appear, at one time, (if we may judge by the action of the Board of Aldermen,) they themselves stood in fear of the police department; instead of being masters and directors, they were the department's pliant tools.

The question is sometimes asked: Can a professional gambler be a good man, or a good citizen? In the common acceptation of the word "good," I answer, most emphatically, yes! I have seen men whose only calling and profession was gaming, who in all their dealings with the world, outside of the gaming table, (I have never seen them there,) were upright and honest. They were good husbands, and good fathers, and were never addicted to the use of intoxicating drinks. They were affable, courteous and gentlemanly, and ever ready to relieve suffering humanity; but you will always find them restless, uneasy beings, men who cannot live out of the whirlpool of excitement.

Where however, you will find such a one as I have described, you will find scores who are exactly the reverse; and happy is that man, who having launched his bark upon the sea of life, so watches the compass and the chart, that he is able to detect the decoy lights which are set on every reef and quicksand bar, to allure him to destruction.

"Now," says I, "Uncle Zeb, I want you to tell me the peculiar characteristics of that man."

"I will do so," he replied, "this evening, after we return home."

The old gentleman drew from his pocket a small note-book, and therein inserted the names of the clerks and the different police officers who were directly connected with this court. He watched them all very carefully, and on the following evening he thus spoke of the

HON. J. G. ROGERS.

"I know not where Judge Rogers was born, nor who his ancestors were, or what his antecedents are; but he appears to me like a singular, odd, and rather eccentric man. I should think he was born for no other purpose save and except to fill the position he now occupies; and I question much whether you could find another position in society, in which to place him, where he could by any possibility 'act well his part,' unless it was in the pulpit. It is barely possible, that if he was placed there, and clothed in the sacerdotal robes, he might occasionally turn a sinner from the errors of his ways; but he never would become popular with the fashionable congregations of the present day. Possibly, had he not been promoted to the 'Bench,' he might have made an excellent counsellor at law; but no son or daughter of 'Momus' would ever dare to enter the precincts of his office—all of his clients would be staid, melancholy and misanthropic. He moves among the busy scenes of life, but appears to take no interest or pleasure in them. I believe that one good, hearty, side-shaking laugh, would consign him to the tomb of his fore-fathers, as quickly as a powerful narcotic. It is true that his countenance is sometimes lighted up with a serene and benignant smile, but as it passes away, and a gloomy cloud o'er-shadows his face, a casual observer would be led to exclaim, 'chaos is come again.'

I am inclined to believe that Judge Rogers is a kind and affectionate friend, an upright lawgiver, a conscientious and honest man."

After Uncle Zeb had finished his brief description of Judge Rogers, I prevailed upon him to give me an outline, or physiological chart, of another well-known Justice, whom Uncle Zeb had seen two or three times—the

HON. ABEL CUSHING.

"In Judge Cushing," said Uncle Zeb, "you will find the most curious compound that was ever yet moulded together into the form of a man. He is an anamoly; and I opine that the shrewdest observers would necessarily be obliged to watch him for a long time, before they could fully comprehend his character sufficiently to form a correct and unbiased opinion of the man.

He is undoubtedly well versed in all law matters that

appertain directly to the court over which he presides; and being a very cautious man, he does not despatch business quite so rapidly as some who have come upon the stage since he made his *debut*, and it is very evident that he cannot appreciate the active business movements of some younger men, who despatch business rapidly, in this exceedingly fast age.

There is one thing which is highly commendable in Justice Cushing: that is, his fixed determination to protect the rights of every prisoner who is brought before him, however poor or degraded they may be. If a prisoner has no counsel, or witnesses for the defence, he will postpone the trial, if by so doing they can obtain either. He has too much of the milk of human kindness in his composition to sentence a man first, and try him afterwards.

When a couple of 'scrub lawyers' get hold of a two and sixpenny case, which is to be tried before Justice Cushing, it is sometimes amusing to see with what martyr-like resignation the old gentleman will set and listen to the verbose harangues which these noddle-headed, self-styled attornies call unanswerable arguments.

When these declaimers begin to argue a case, our Justice will set with his chin resting upon his hands, looking intently at the two lawyers. The workings of his mind, as indicated by his countenance, seemed to say: 'Nature's journeymen manufactured those pedantic lawyers, and an abominable job they made of it.' He will then 'strait'en up,' as the Yankee comedians say, and commence:

'Well, gentlemen, I have listened very attentively to your arguments, and I'm glad you've got through. The argument of the counsel for the prosecution would be very excellent, provided that there ever was a law enacted in the State of Massachusetts, like the one alluded to by him. I believe there is such a law now extant on the Statute Books, in the State of Rhode Island, but that, of course, will not answer our turn. The counsel for the defendant cites from reports of trials which were held in this State, under a similar law, that was in existence here. But that law has been repealed ten or twelve years.'

Although Justice C. has a retentive memory in matters of law, he cannot recollect names and faces. Oftentimes this is a source of annoyance and perplexity to him.

On one occasion, when a case of assault and battery was brought before him to adjudicate upon, among the witnesses called up, there was a tall, spare-featured man, whose locks had been whitened by the snows of seventy winters; his dress and general appearance denoted a gentleman of the old school. During his examination he was very exact and concise in all his answers. When asked whether the parties on trial ever had any altercation before. He replied: Yes; but I cannot recollect whether it was previous to my going south, or since my return from the south.

The worthy Judge inquired: "When did you go south, and how long did you remain?'

The old man looked quaintly at the Judge, as he replied: 'Your Honor's memory is not very good, I perceive. I only remained three months; just three months! Your Honor sent me there, to live at the city's expense, in the House of Correction; I never traveled farther south than that. I marvel your worship has forgotten the circumstance; I never shall, you may be sure of that!'

'Probably not!' replied the Justice, who had unconsciously joined in the merriment which this speech had occasioned in the court-room. 'I hope I never shall have occasion to consign you to that place again!'

'By the Eternal!' shouted the witness, 'those were the last words you repeated to me, when you sent me traveling south, some four months ago!'

The whole court was convulsed with laughter, and it was some time before order could be restored.

Having devoted all the space that I can spare to this respected and worthy man, I will leave him, and glance at the junior Justice of the Boston Police Court,

HON. THOMAS RUSSELL.

This gentleman was born in Plymouth, Mass., in 1825, graduated at Cambridge, in 1845, and commenced practicing law in 1850. He was twenty-seven years of age when he was appointed to the position which he now occupies, consequently he had but two years practice as an advocate at the "Bar." His appointment was considered by some as impolitic and injudicious ; nevertheless, he has proved himself amply competent, and notwithstanding the assertions made by a certain chief magistrate, that he had "soiled the ermine." This assertion was never substantiated by proof or testimony.

It is true that he is a young man, but it is also true that he gives his time and undivided attention to his professional duties. If upon the Bench he does not assume the gravity of the "Philosopher's Owl," his decisions are for the most part in strict accordance with law, justice and equity.

When Justice Russell is upon the Bench, witnesses should be exceedingly careful how they testify. If they come with a lie in their mouths, the chances are that they will become prisoners, instead of witnesses, and be sent up to a higher court, indicted for perjury.

Some of his decisions are hastily made, and many persons think, ill-timed ; be that as it may, he is considered by the community at large to be an upright magistrate, and an impartial dispenser of the law."

"Now," says I, "Uncle Zeb, let us look at that restless gentleman, who sits directly in front of the Justice's Bench, with gold-bowed spectacles upon his nose. That is the worthy Clerk of the Court,

THOMAS POWER, ESQ.

Mr. Power has filled the office which he now occupies thirty-four years. He was born in the city of Boston, in an old wooden building, on Hanover, near the corner of Union street, hard by the tallow-chandler's establishment where Benjamin Franklin was employed, previous to his entering a printing-office. He made his advent October the 8th, 1786; consequently he is now in the seventy-eighth year of his age.

Old Father Time has dealt very gently with Mr. Power. He appears to walk as erect, and shows as much activity and vivacity as he did thirty years ago. He can fasten a pair of skates upon his feet, and skim over the frozen lake, out-distancing every beardless boy, and most of the athletic and practised skaters.

Mr. Power graduated at Brown University, in 1808, and commenced the practice of law, shortly afterwards, in Northfield, where he remained several years.

In the Court House, Mr. P. is altogether a different man from what you find him outside. In his desk he is austere, fractious and irritable, especially when he is annoyed by those "scrubs" who have the glaring impudence to call themselves lawyers, or some pseudo-philanthropist, who is prowling about, wolf-like, in sheep's clothing, and with their hypocritical cant applying their "pickers and stealers" to the pockets of the goats, while at the same time they keep an eye upon the ewes and lambs of the flock. Mr. Power has had such opportunities to watch the doings of these vampires, that when one of them approaches him, to bore and annoy him, fever and fits are sure to follow. A true, noble-hearted philanthropist, whose sole end and aim is to elevate the human race, will always find in him a ready supporter and willing co-operator; but it is the land-sharks and hypocrites he despises.

In the common walks of life, Mr. P. is one of the most pleasing, polite and affable men that can be found in the city. His open hand and genial heart are ever ready to welcome a friend, or receive a stranger; in fact, his society is courted by the intellectual and good, of all classes.

In "Loring's" "One Hundred Orators of Boston," Mr. Power is counted in "one." I never saw the gentleman upon the rostrum, but I have not a very exalted idea of his oratorical endowments. He can wield the pen better than he can use his tongue, as a musical critic he has few, if any superiors.

Mr. P. has written many poems of a superior order. Some of them will live long after the author has passed that bourne from whence no traveller returns. We will now glance at the amiable, good natured, and ever pleasing Assistant Clerk of the Police Court,

SETH TOBY, ESQ.

This gentleman is a native of Barnstable, Mass., a town noted as being the birth-place of Chief Justice Shaw, and other distinguished New England men.

Mr. T. was appointed Assistant Clerk of the Police Court in 1848 and has retained the situation up to the present time. His appointment was a very excellent and judicious one; few men could be found better qualified to fill the office.

Mr. T. was educated at Cambridge, and studied law with the late Robert Rantoul, Jr., while that gentleman held the office of United States District Attorney. Mr. Rantoul found his young student to be one in whose correctness and integrity he could place the strictest confidence.

Indictments, and legal documents which required great care in drawing up, were entrusted to him, and in one case, where there were three indictments, containing each twenty-four counts, not one error was found, nor one indictment quashed for informality.

Thus it appears Mr. Toby is somewhat of an attorney withal. Long may he live to fill the situation which he now holds.

It is with great pleasure that I am enabled to introduce to the public another very important officer of the courts of Boston :

DR. ISAAC WORSLEY.

The Doctor is not a proud or vain-glorious man. There are only three things of which he boasts; the first is : that his father fought at the battle of Bunker Hill, and was but a few paces from General Warren when that hero and patriot fell. The second is : the beauty and convenience of his carriage, together with the sleekness and high mettle of his pair of thorough bred nags. His third boast is : the wonderful efficacy of a salve which he himself prepares and applies freely to some of his patients. He believes (and I have no reason to doubt it,) that all other salves invented and compounded would bear no more comparison with his, than the glimmering of a taper to the bright rays of the noon-day sun.

Seven times and seven have I besought the Doctor to bestow upon me a modicum of this precious ointment, but I have never as yet received a particle.

The Doctor always wears a serene and placid countenance. When "Gray" wrote his "Elegy in a churchyard," he must have had in his mind's eye such a one as the Doctor ; else he never would have written :

"Melancholy marked him for her own."

But, in truth, the Doctor is not a melancholy man,

DR. ISAAC WORSLEY

(See Page 104.)

he is only engaged in a melancholy business. Who expects to see a sexton laughing and grinning while he is engaged in consigning the mortal remains of some departed one to the tomb? How much less, then, should the Doctor indulge in cachinnations, while he is engaged in conveying his fellow-beings, not singly, but in battalions, to a living tomb?

The idea itself is perfectly preposterous!

We have before stated that the Doctor drove a magnificent span of horses. Not long since the Assistant Clerk of the Police Court circulated a story respecting the Doctor, which was annoying to him; but no one who knew the man believed there was one word of truth in the statement, the substance of which was as follows:

At a certain time, when the Doctor and the said Clerk were discussing the merits and demerits of the aforesaid team, the Doctor, in an unguarded moment, offered to wager ten dollars that he could drive his team, in a light wagon, ten miles in three hours, provided the road was level, and in good order.

The Clerk accepted the wager, and insisted upon his making the trial.

But the Doctor "caved in,"—he "backed out." Afterwards, while conversing with a friend, in a serious mood, respecting the matter, he remarked: "O! I could do it, but it might injure the animals!"

On one occasion as he was driving down Broadway,

(South Boston,) a strange gentleman hailed him, with the usual inquiry:

"All full inside?"

"Yes, sir," was the response.

"Well, as I am in something of a hurry, I'll get up and ride with you."

The gentleman jumped on with the driver, and when they arrived at the head of State street, the passenger signified his intention to stop, and inquired what fare was demanded?

"Nothing, sir," was the reply.

"How is that?" inquired the stranger. "Is not this a public omnibus?"

"Public enough," was the response. "This is the 'Black Maria,' and is used to convey passengers from the Court House to the House of Correction."

The passenger incontinently "mizzled."

The Doctor is a man who possesses a kind heart. Many times and oft, when some poor, unfortunate being has been handed over to him, he has furnished them with food, and paid for it out of his own private purse. This fact was made known to the Directors of the House of Correction, and he was told by one of them to give him the amount he had so expended. The reply was:

"What I have done was done on my own responsibility, and I ask no remuneration."

I trust that the Doctor will not become weary in well

doing, "for in due season he will reap, if he faints not."

Let us now pass to the oldest officer in the Police Court:

JONAS STRATTON.

We have no engraving of this gentleman, know nothing of his birth, ancestry, or antecedents. He has been in the Police Court of Boston, in the capacity of an officer, for many years, and I presume he would not have retained the situation, unless he had given good satisfaction to all parties during his term of service.

Mr. S. was in his younger days a very strong, athletic man; and even now, after Old Time has shorn off some of his locks, he is able to cope successfully with any man who does not possess more than ordinary strength. He is an active and industrious man, who well understands how, when, and where to look after the main chances, while playing his cards in the great game of life.

We will now turn to another well known Police Court officer:

JACOB C. TALLANT.

This man came to the city of Boston, from his native place, the town of Errol, New Hampshire, about thirty-two years ago. He came on foot, with all the spare clothes he had, tied up in a bandanna handkerchief, and three dollars cash in his pocket.

Where he first obtained a situation, or what business he followed for some years afterwards, I know not.

He was appointed an officer in and for the Police Court of Boston in the year 1840, which situation he has retained since that time.

In 1847, Mr. Tallant was offered a better and more lucrative office than the one which he now holds. This he most respectfully declined, saying: "I know what I am, but I know not what I may be."

As a court officer, Mr. T. is courteous and polite. He makes many friends, and but few enemies.

He has always been in favor of any, and every proposed reform which would tend to ameliorate the hardships and sufferings of the unfortunate prisoners, both in the Police and higher courts, and was never yet known to deal harshly with a prisoner, unless absolutely compelled so to do.

Mr. T. does not entertain a very exalted opinion of "scrub lawyers," or "two penny philanthropists." The first class of suckers, he thinks, are generally sure to send the prisoner "up;" the other will send the prisoner "over;" so that in either case the victim is victimized, the moment he falls into their hands.

Mr. T. thinks that both classes of those imps who hang around the Court House are gifted with "second sight." He says they can look into every man's pocket, and if they see no money there, it is impossible for them to see the prisoner ; but if they do discover two, three, or five dollars, as the case may be, they are sure to "fob" it. But then we must bear in mind that Mr. T. is slightly tinctured with what is called old fogyism ; and it cannot be expected that he can appreciate the motives of those *benevole* and erratic gentlemen.

There are but few men among our police officers who enjoy a greater share of the respect and esteem of their fellow-citizens, than the man, Jacob C. Tallant.

The next Police Court officer whose integrity, patriotism and virtue demands a brief notice, is

SAMUEL S. VIALLE.

It has often been a query in the minds of some, whether it is possible for a man who associates with vicious and abandoned characters for a long time, to retain his good qualities, and not be contaminated. I think such a thing may be possible, although "a man is generally known by the company he keeps." If this maxim holds good in every case, Mr. Vialle must necessarily be one of the worst men in the community. I have seen him advising with, and assisting thieves, house-breakers, incendiaries and murderers, and he never appears to feel ashamed to be seen in their company. He says that there are two rules or codes of laws which govern mankind. God gave us the first, which is : "Do unto others as you would have others do unto you." Man made the second, which is in some respects similar to the first, and which, when deviated from, will limit the area of the transgressor's freedom, and bring him into close contact with iron bars and bracelets.

Mr. Vialle is a calm, self-possessed man, of an amiable and obliging disposition, but occasionally you can see a little of the old Adam light up in his eye. How can a man remain cool and calm, when some vagabond spits in his face, or when he sees a desperado making preparations to knock him down? On such occasions, self-preservation will become the ruling passion.

Mr. Vialle was appointed an officer of the Police Court in 1843, and has retained the office since that time. He is a very unassuming man, ever diligent in business, as he labors in the service of the Commonwealth.

WILLIAM BLAISDELL.

The appointment of Mr. B. as a Police Court officer is of recent date. He is one of the most quiet men that can be found in the community. There is no noise, no bustle, and but little excitement to be seen in him, either in, or out of the Court House. He has done the State some service, previous to his appointment to his present position. He fought in the battles of Mexico, in the army, under General Taylor, and is familiar with scenes of blood and carnage. He is no stranger to want, privation and suffering. If I have not been misinformed, he was severely (at the time it was supposed mortally) wounded, in one of the Mexican battles. He has the appearance of a brave, but not a reckless man. He is about forty-five years of age, and I believe he is an exemplary court officer.

I will now sketch the last officer on the list, who is a very handsome man, and one who must be seen to be properly appreciated. The engraved likeness of the gentleman, which can be found on another page, has been pronounced to be a great deal *better* looking than the original, or a great deal *worse*, I don't recollect which.

ELIJAH K. SPOOR.

"Hamlet," when he spoke of his defunct paternal parent, boldly asserted that "he was a man," and then expressed his honest belief that he should "never look upon his like again." Some express the same opinion respecting Mr. S., and I am inclined to the belief that more than one generation will pass away before the inhabitants of this mundane sphere will have an opportunity to look upon another like him.

There are but few men better qualified for the situation which he holds than Mr. S. He received his appointment in 1849, and still remains in office. He is a man of strong impulses, but is generally kind and considerate in his dealings with prisoners. He is a liberal man; I do not think there is a particle of meanness in his composition. He is a bustling, active man, withal, and his stentorian voice is often heard in the court-room, shouting, "Take off your hat!—Stop talking in Court!—Silence!—All those who have no business in Court will please to leave, in double-quick time!—Make that man with the white hat and yellow dickey sit down, or else put him out! Mr. Philanthropist, let that 'cullud gal' alone till after her trial, 'cause you annoy the court and the gal too!"—and such like exclamations.

When not on duty, Mr. S. is a very social, companionable man, his smiling phiz and hearty laugh would startle an anchorite from his propriety. No man enjoys a good joke better than himself, while his keen susceptibility of the ludicrous is such that when relating a story or anecdote, he can draw upon his imagination for all the embelishments they may require.

To sum up the whole matter, Mr. Spoor is a good officer, and we find in his character many excellent traits.

CHAPTER VII.

Court Reporters—Their influence for good or for evil—Their comicalities and erratic movements—Their sympathies for old friends in trouble, especially unfortunate typoes—Examination of a law student—A Reporter's stratagem—A venerable colored Deacon in the Police Court, trying to identify some of his deceased wife's garments,

THE next important personages in and about the Court House are the "Reporters" of the public press. Wherever they move their influence is felt, for good or for evil; and whenever one of them puts before the public a partial or garbled account of any transaction or scenes enacted in the Court House, or elsewhere, they are liable to do incalculable injury to individuals, as well as to others with whom such individuals may be connected.

The reporters of the public press of Boston, New-York and Philadelphia, are, for the most part, gentlemen, in the strictest sense of the term. Although I do not suppose that they are an associated body, (secret or otherwise,) they appear to be bound together by a sort of mystic tie. Whenever a "snob" or "muff" creeps in among them, he is sure to get the cold shoulder. The regular reporter will never associate with one of this class ; and one might as well try to " ride a camel—yea, leap him flying through a needle's eye," as to attempt to palm himself off as a reporter, among the regular reportorial fraternity.

There is nothing that a man who lays any claim to respectability or fair standing in the community dreads more, if he happens to find himself in court, for some transgression of the law, or violation of a city ordinance, than the reporters. I have often seen men who were arraigned for some trivial offence, go to the reporters, and with tears in their eyes beg of them not to mention their names in the court reports ; and I have seen others who would attempt to bribe them. I once saw a man, who, after his examination, and the imposition of a fine, went to the reporters, and publicly offered them money to suppress a report of the case. Every legitimate reporter refused the proffered bribe, and then not only reported the case in full, but gave the gentleman " a first-rate notice," stating the whole affair, the amount of money offered to suppress it, &c.

Now if this man had spoken to one of the corps, and requested him to communicate with his associates, and have the report suppressed, it would unquestionably have been done ; but he took the wrong course, and brought ridicule upon himself.

Whenever an old " typo," or any one who is or has been connected with a printing-office, happens to violate that commandment which reads : "Thou shalt not drink too much intoxicating liquor ;" and is brought into court to answer the charge, if the man is without money, the reporters will draw their wallets, pay the fine, and send the unfortunate home.

I knew a reporter, who, on some occasions, would volunteer his services, and act as counsel for the prisoners, when he thought they were poor and oppressed. In most instances he would gain his case, and get his client acquitted.

One day he volunteered to defend an old woman who had "just arrived from swate Ireland." She was charged with purloining goods from a store at the north part of the city. Our *soi-disant* lawyer undertook her case, but he soon found that the chances were decidedly against him. When he saw how matters stood, he stepped out ; for what purpose, is none of my business, nor yours, kind reader. The Judge, before passing sentence, asked the usual question :

"Have you anything to say respecting your sentence ?"

The woman, finding herself deserted by her lawyer, undertook to plead her own case, which she wound up by exclaiming : "I call upon God to witness that I am innocent, intirely !"

The worthy Clerk, who had been very busily engaged in filing his documents, without paying the least attention to the harangue of the accused, only heard a part of the last sentence: "I call upon—witness—innocent intirely."

He rose up in his desk, and said:

"Woman! if your witness is in court, bring him up, and have him sworn."

The poor culprit stood aghast, the Judge appeared to be troubled with a cholic, and suddenly disappeared through the side-door. The officers were convulsed with laughter, while the Clerk, and those spectators who had not heard the woman's speech, were amazed and wondered at the indecorous proceedings.

Afterwards, when our philanthropic attorney in this case was informed of the sequel, he shook his head, and gravely remarked:

"Ah! I'm sorry I didn't remain. Had I been there, I should have claimed a postponement until the prisoner could produce her witness for the defence, and thereby prove her innocence."

I have known instances where court reporters, who have emigrated to the southern and western sections of the continent, have there been elected by the people judges and lawgivers. In such cases these promoted ones will generally administer justice without much regard to the law.

Let one of them remain a few years on the borders of our frontiers, and they will get so accustomed to the tastes, manners and habits of the people, that they will become like them. This must necessarily follow; it is for their interest to think and act as their constituents would have them. They must be dignified, but their dignity must be democratic dignity, which they can put on as they would their coat, when they take their seat upon the Bench; but they are expected to drop it, when they get outside the Court House; and if they happen into the bar-room of a log-cabin tavern, where the plaintiff or defendant, with their friends, are congregated, they are expected to treat the crowd, if they have decided the case against them. If otherwise, every person concerned is bound to treat the Judge, or, as they term it, put him through a regular "course of sprouts." This is their custom, and with them, custom makes the law.

I have previously spoken of pettifogging lawyers, and the *modus operandi* of gaining admission to practice at the bar, in the Middle and Eastern States. In the Southern and Western States, it is far different. Every applicant who aspires to the honor of carrying the green bag, and be acknowledged as an attorney, must be examined by the Judge, personally. Whether this is an improvement upon the practice at the east, I will leave the reader to judge for himself, after he has read the subjoined examination of a law-student.

A young man, who had received a liberal education, and finished his law studies, concluded to emigrate to the western part of Illinois, to settle and commence his practice.

At that time the population of the country, in that section, was rather thin, and people having law-business to transact were obliged to travel many miles to reach a Court House. The taverns and Temples of Justice in the shire towns were nothing more than log-cabins, and very poorly furnished at that.

Our young attorney, after his arrival, waited for some time for the first court session, when he was to undergo an examination by the Circuit Judge.

He was informed that the Judge of that circuit was one of the hardest old "hosses" that could be found in the "diggins," and that he generally "put it" to young applicants in the "awfullest way."

Our candidate looked anxiously forward to the day when he would be obliged to pass through the fiery ordeal. He re-examined "Coke" and "Blackstone," together with other equally important law-books.

The Judge at length arrived. He was a short, thick-set, burly looking man, adout fifty years of age, and his rubicund countenance and "Bardolph" nose clearly indicated that if he had ever joined a temperance society, it must have been a long time ago; and that himself and the whiskey bottle had been inseparable friends for many years, whatever his talents might have been as a law expounder and dispenser.

The law student introduced himself to his Honor, and made known the object of his visit.

"Whar did you come from?" inquired the Judge, eyeing the student from head to foot, with a scrutinizing glance.

"From Massachusetts, your Honor," was the reply.

"Well! you just come into the tavern after the court adjourns, and then I'll see how your corporation rich-er-osh-er-gasher-ates."

At the time appointed the law-student found himself in the log-tavern, seated with the Judge at a small table; and the first question the Judge asked, was:

"Stranger, how 're you on't for funds?"

"I have some money left," was the reply.

"Good! Landlord, pass along a bottle of that old whiskey!" shouted the Judge.

And as it was brought before him, he poured out a bumper, and swallowing it at one draught, remarked to his companion:

"Stranger, I'm glad to see you, d—d if I aint. Now I'll proceed to examine you, stranger.

"In the first place, I want to know whether you are a married man or not?"

Student. "I am not a married man, sir."

Judge. "Good! I'm glad on't. A man who expects to get a living by practising law, don't need a wife no more than a big bull-dog needs a tin-kettle tied to his tail, not a bit; but come, stranger, let's take another drink."

Student. "With all my heart, sir."

Judge. "And now, stranger, I want to ask you a very important question: Do you own a horse?"

Student. "Yes, sir, and a good one it is.

Judge. "Well, stranger, the more I see of you, the better I like you. I shouldn't be so particular in examining you, but you see the law requires it! Let's take another drink! Well, now, I will proceed, and I want you to answer my questions just as if you was under oath. My next question is: Can you swim?"

Student. "Yes, sir, I can swim"

Judge. "Good! I was cursed 'fraid you couldn't; I consider a man who can't swim jest no man at all. Now you say you've got a horse, and you can swim; now I have got to ask you a very important question: Can your horse swim?"

Student. "Yes, sir, he can."

Judge. "How do you know that, sir?"

Student. "Because I have tried him."

Judge. "Good again! Let's take another drink; and I'll make out your papers so you can have them tomorrow morning. I find you're O. K., and will make a glorious lawyer."

Whether this style of examination is an improvement upon the plan which is adopted in Massachusetts, we shall not attempt to decide, but let the reader judge for himself.

I will now return to the court reporters. The major part of them are "fellows of infinite jest, of most excellent fancy." They have made me laugh a thousand times at their sly pranks, witticisms and manœuvres in a court room. When a colored individual is arraigned for some minor offence, they always seem determined to have a little sport among themselves, and sometimes it is at the expense of the court. I well recollect a case in point:

A young mulatto girl was brought up charged with having been found in a house of ill-fame, on which the police had made a descent the previous night. One of the reporters having seen the girl on a former occasion, at a negro concert, and knowing that she was possessed of a sweet and melodious voice, also knowing full well that the worthy Clerk had a great penchant for music, he stepped round where she was seated, and whispered to her something like this:

"When you are brought on to the stand, and the Clerk asks you whether you are guilty or not, sing some plaintive or mournful song."

The girl profited by this advice, and when she was brought upon the stand, to hear the complaint read against her, she stood as motionless as a statue. The Clerk rather tartly asked:

"Are you guilty, or not guilty?"

The girl turned her dark blue eyes upward, and with a voice of the sweetest accents, and most melodious notes commenced from that well-known German song:

"Thou, thou, know'st that I love thee;"

The venerable Justice scratched the musical bump of his venerable head. The Clerk stood gazing at the prisoner with wondering astonishment, and the officers, witnesses and spectators appeared for the moment paralyzed; even officer Spoor himself forgot his cue, and neglected to shout, as usual, "Order in the Court." The Clerk, resuming his dignity, again asked the question, "Are you guilty, or not guilty?"

The fair respondent faintly replied: "Not guilty," and immediately put her vocal powers into action again, singing:—

"Let me go where fate may lead me,
Let me cross yon troubled deep;
Where no stranger ear shall greet me,
Where no eye for me shall weep."

The Clerk threw down the complaint, and as he proceeded to call the witnesses, he uttered the sentence, *sotto voce*:

"That woman can't be guilty of any *crime!*"

The officers testified very lightly against her, and there was no evidence to prove that she was one of the household. The woman was immediately discharged, and the pocket of our reporter, who concocted the plan, was relieved of several dimes, by his brother reporters, at the first restorant they came to, on their return to the printing-offices.

There is in the city of Boston, a gentleman of color, by the name of "Foster." He is well known to most of our citizens as the most aristocratic and dignified colored gentleman of all his "race." He boasts of having been Aid-de-camp to every Governor since the days of a blessed good Governor, whose name he can't recollect, no how, without examining the documents. The reporters always bestow upon him a large amount of fulsome praise, except when he happens to be called into Court, and then their custom is (perhaps the custom would be "more honored in the breach than in the observance,") to report his speeches and testimony verbatim. This most excellent and respectable gentleman glories in the *soubriquet* of "Deacon;" but whether he is in reality the deacon of any church, or otherwise, I have never yet been informed.

A short time ago the deacon appeared in the Police Court, and entered a complaint against a cullurd lady, whom he had caught in the act of embezzling, feloniously taking, with malice aforethought, carrying away, and appropriating to her own use, certain garments, once belonging to his own beloved, but defunct wife; but now his own lawful property; against the laws and statutes of the State of Massachusetts, in such case made and provided.

The deacon appeared in court with the officer who seized the goods pointed out as purloined. He had no witnesses, save and except himself. Why should he? The gentleman who had served seven Governors, not one of whom ever doubted his word, did not need any corroborating testimony to satisfy the Judge of a *petite* court that he was a man of honor. The articles alleged to be purloined consisted of shawls, dresses, capes, petticoats, chemises, and other articles of ladies' wearing apparel, which I will not mention, because I do not understand to what use they are applied. The deacon was called upon the stand, and a paraphernalia of linen, cotton, woolen and silk was placed before him, for identification. According to the statements made by the wicked reporters, the deacon, after carefully examining the garments, amused, if he did not instruct the court, in giving his testimony. He commenced thus:

"Dar, you see, dis am my wife's night-cap; I know dat cap, wheneber I sees it. I knows jest as well when she made dat cap as nothin! Ah, dar's dat chemise, too; I'se seen dat more an a hundred times! Ah, what's de melancholy feelings dat come ober me, ebry time I look at dat chemise!"

Here the deacon almost shed tears, as he took a retrospective glance at the happy hours which were forever past, but which that chemise brought to his fond remembrance.

The Judge, who was inexperienced in such matters, blushed, and was for a moment slightly confused. He evidently did not relish the idea of taking up the chemise, (the case, I mean,) either for the use of the plaintiff or defendant. It was very apparent that he could not appreciate the utility of the article in question; but when he gained his equilibrium, he asked the deacon if there was any mark upon the chemise, whereby he could identify it?

"Mark enough!" responded the deacon, "I knows de marks; and den dar's dat shawl, I know's dat shawl well enough, dat shawl was my wife's, and no mistake."

"Is there any mark upon the shawl whereby you can identify that?" inquired his Honor.

"Yes, sah," replied the deacon, getting somewhat excited. "My wife's sister's got one jest 'zactly like it, and if you put them both together, you couldn't tell one from the oder. Guess I knows well enough when I sees dat shawl! it's a real nice one, cost tree dollars.

"I don't think you've made out a case of larceny here, Mr. Foster, because you cannot identify any article alleged to have been stolen," quoth the Judge.

"'Dentify! 'dentify!" shouted the deacon; "I 'dentify ebry ting dat's here, and good many oder tings which I can't find, if I on'y finds um, I'll 'dentify um."

The prisoner was discharged; and as the deacon saw his cherished articles handed over to her, he gave a long, drawn sigh, and as he left the court room he cast more than one

> "Longing, lingering, look behind."

I find that I have slighted my antique and worthy relative, Uncle Zeb, not having mentioned or alluded to him for some time. The truth is, it is impossible for me to keep step with the old man. He wants to stop and consider for a long time before he expresses an opinion; *I* want to propel under double steam pressure, but I sometimes find it necessary to "draw up" and consult the old gentleman. In my subsequent chapters, I shall be obliged to advise with him, as I chronicle some past events.

CHAPTER VIII.

Courts in the city of Philadelphia—Corruption among the New York Officials—The citizens of Boston easily humbugged—Coroners and Coroners' Juries—The Country Coroner, with his Jury of Fishermen—Justices of the Peace—The advantage of holding a Justice's Commission—Court Rooms in Country Towns—A new style of administering an Oath—A New Hampshire Justice soliciting an Office from President Pierce.

In the State of Pennsylvania, especially in the city of Philadelphia, we find a marked difference between the arraignments and conducting of courts there, than of those in other States and cities.

In the Philadelphia courts, the Quaker gravity is still maintained by many of the attorneys, officers and witnesses, as well as with the Judge upon the Bench, notwithstanding the rowdyism of its firemen, and the frequent broils, quarrels and fights which so often occur in the city proper and adjoining districts.

Although we there find a few of those pests termed pettifogging lawyers, they are not very numerous. The reason of this is, the people, even those of the poorest class, will not patronize them, (or perhaps the climate does not agree with them,) and they are obliged to seek a sustenance in other quarters, where their talents and genius will be appreciated. Probably there is no city in the Union where the courts are conducted with more propriety, or freer from corruption, than those of the Quaker city.

How different it is when we look at New York city, and see how the courts are there managed. There corruption runs riot; Judges become accomplices of notorious thieves and murderers, while the subordinate officers of the court act as go-betweens, and share with them the plunder and booty.

In New York city a second or third rate lawyer can reach a Judge's Bench, if he has a little smattering of law, and is a noisy, brawling, political demagogue. It matters not what his antecedents are, because honesty and capability are no tests with the dominant party of that corrupt city. In proof of this, I refer the reader to the court reports, as published in the newspapers of the day, for the past five years. In these we have records of the trials of Judges who have been in intimate connection with, and received bribes from, notorious robbers, to large amounts, while the court officers of lower grades, and the Police department, (taken as many of them were, from low bar-rooms and gambling hells,) were adepts in the science of compounding felony.

In a previous chapter I have said, that the present efficient Mayor of New York city has done much to cor-

SAMUEL S. VIALLE.

(See Page 109.)

rect these abuses, and eradicate the many evils which he found amongst the city officials when he came into office. He soon discovered that he had an herculean task before him, and that these "Augean stables" could not be cleansed in a day; and the only wonder is that instead of attempting a reformation, he did not turn back in despair, and exclaim, like one of old: "Ephraim is joined to his idols, let him alone."

I have already said that I believed the magistrates of Massachusetts, from the Chief Justice down to those who occupy minor stations upon the Bench, are for the most part men of probity, who do as much honor to the station they occupy, as the robes of office honor them. It is true that a certain Governor did openly declare that one of the Judges had "soiled the ermine," but this assertion has never yet been substantiated by any proof; and it is also true that the Massachusetts Legislature, in 1855, labored strenuously to impeach the Hon. C. G. Loring, one of the United States District Judges, because he would not violate his oath of office at the bidding of a party of hot-brained fanatics, who are always ready to engender strife, when by so doing an opportunity offers to bring their names before the public. But the reader will bear in mind that the (so called) Legislature of 1855, taken collectively, were a very peculiar set of men. Many of them have become more enlightened since the body adjourned, and now, in their closets, upon the house-tops, and at the corners of the streets, they cry, "Lord, pardon thy servant, in this thing."

The citizens of Boston are more easily excited and humbugged than the denizens of any other place in the States. They are always eager to see or hear some new thing. If an announcement was made that a man with cropped ears and a long red beard would preach in St. Paul's church, at a specified time, the church would be crowded long before the services commenced. If some humbug Count or Prince comes among them, thousands will rush to see him. Members of the city government will wait upon him, to tender him a grand banquet, while the mechanic will leave his work-shop, and the poor day-laborer his toil, and all, in one heterogeneous mass, rush to see and do honor to the "Illustrious stranger." *

Methinks I hear the reader say, you had better drop this subject, before you get into deep water, where your little bark will get swamped, and confine yourself to courts and court officers.

* Many of our readers will recollect that in 1851 a shrewd, cunning Turk, who had been entrusted with a few documents, which were of themselves but of little importance, came here, and represented himself as a Grand Embassador from his "Imperial Highness, the Grand Sultan of Turkey." He was feted and banqueted. If I mistake not, one of the 1855 Senators expended several hundred dollars in preparing a feast for this distinguished humbug; and probably it was for that reason alone the citizens of a *free State* placed him in office.

There is one class of officers, who are connected with the courts, directly and indirectly, who would feel aggrieved and insulted, if I should pass them without a brief notice, viz.: Coroners and Coroners' Juries.

These functionaries are, or, at least, they consider themselves, very important men. As they have no stated salaries, their dependance for a livelihood depends entirely upon the accidents and mishaps which befall their fellow men. When some unfortunate, weary of the world, severs "life's brittle thread," by taking a cold bath, or testing the strength of a rope, by affixing one end of it to a spike, and fastening the other around his neck, it is a perfect God-send to the Coroners.

If a still-born infant is found in a state of decomposition, in some cellar or garret, the instant the fact is made known to the Coroner, he hastens to the place, to make an investigation.

In towns and cities where there is more than one Coroner, rivalry often exists between them, and as in "barber's shops," "first come, first served;" and although I do not believe that when two or more of them hear of an accident or sudden death at one and the same time, they would make a regular stampede for the scene of action, I am confident that they will accomplish feats of pedestrianism which would astonish those who imagine that a man cannot walk more than four miles an hour, without injury to his "corporeal corporosity."

When a Coroner hears of two or more cases where his services are required at one and the same time, he will (if he understands his business) start for the nearest subject, and fasten his card upon the body, thereby showing prior claim, in case one of his brother officers should come to it. He will then hasten to secure the next one.

After having secured the body or bodies the Coroner will then proceed to summon a jury. A shrewd Coroner will always use great care in the selection of his jurymen. Strangers, or seafaring men, who are about to start on a long voyage, are preferable to those who reside in the immediate vicinity, for two very obvious reasons, the first of which is that they being totally unacquainted with all parties concerned, will be likely to render a more impartial and unbiased verdict than others who are acquainted with the deceased party or parties. The other reason is, that as the Jurors cannot obtain their fees until the Coroner has drawn them from the County or State treasury, and when he has thus drawn them, there is no law to compel him to hunt up jurymen or witnesses, merely for the sake of tendering them their dues; that Coroner must be an insane man who would harbor the idea of refunding money which was not called for into the treasury. I do not believe there is one Coroner out of fifty who would be guilty of attempting so rash an act.

In the year 1851, I was sojourning, in company with a friend, in a small sea-board town in Essex County, Massachusetts, where I had an opportunity to witness the proceedings at a Coroner's inquest there held. The circumstances connected therewith were as follows:

One very hot, sultry day, in the month of July, an Irishman, who had been but a few days in the country, was at work in a field with three or four others. In the early part of the afternoon, one of the laborers procured a large bucket of ice-water, of which the newly arrived emigrant, while over-heated, drank very freely. The usual results soon followed, and before his companions could obtain any remedies, or convey him to his lodgings, the poor fellow gave up the ghost.

A man was immediately dispatched to notify the Coroner, who lived some three or four miles distant, but some hours elapsed before that functionary arrived at the scene of action.

In company with my friend, (who by the way was a mischievous wag,) we happened to pass the house where the deceased laborer had boarded, and seeing several persons standing in the front yard, who appeared to be considerably excited, we inquired the cause, and after receiving the information, we went in. Presently the Coroner arrived. He was a large, fat, burly old fellow, about sixty years of age, with pomposity and mock-dignity enough to serve the turn of a dozen Coroners, if it could be equally divided between them. He took the witnesses by themselves into a private room, asked them a few questions, then came out, and walking up to my companion, he said :

" Sir, I order you to serve on this jury of inquest."

From some inexplicable cause, he passed me, (perhaps he did not like my looks,) and went directly out into the front yard, where a squad of fishermen were standing, and ordered five of them to serve as jurors. He then wrote their names upon a slip of paper, and returned to the room.

The fishermen were taken all aback ; their schooner lay but a short distance from the place, and they were only waiting for a full tide to proceed on their voyage. They looked and acted as though they wished the Coroner in the place of the dead man, and the dead man several miles off soundings. It was very evident that not one of them had the remotest idea of the duties which would be required of them, or the length of time they would be detained.

" Each in his fellow's face did look, with mute astonishment."

After the six jurymen were seated around a large pine table, the Coroner proceeded to address them :

" Gentlemen," said he, " this is a solemn occasion, and it brings an awful warning. There lays that ere man, who eat his breakfast well enough this morning, though they say he didn't have much appetite for his dinner; and now he is dead. Now what I have summoned you for, is to have you inquire among these ere witnesses, and find out how that ere man come to die. I've talked to 'em, and am satisfied well enough myself that he cum to his death for no other reason than drinking too much *cold* water with *ice* in it. But you may go and talk to 'em, all of you that want to, and I'll write out a verdict, then you'll all sign your names to it, and take an oath, and that's all you've got to do."

The countenances of the fishermen brightened up. They imagined that in less than fifteen minutes the business would be brought to a close, and they would be allowed to depart. The poor fellows were doomed to be sorely disappointed.

While the fishermen were talking with the witnesses, and the Coroner writing out a verdict, my companion, who sat at the opposite side of the table, was gazing at the Coroner with a serio-comical look, and it was very evident to my mind that there was mischief brewing, and that the pompous functionary who then supposed that everything was "*all right*," would presently find out that everything was "*all wrong*."

When the fishermen were re-seated at the table, and the Coroner had finished his document, he read it to them, and handed it to the one nearest to him, on his right, who signed it, as did two others; but when it came to my companion, he looked at it for a moment, and then exclaimed:

"In Heaven's name! what's this?"

"That is the verdict of the jury," replied the Coroner. "I thought you all understood it well enough when I read it."

"Well, I shan't sign anything of that kind!" said my companion.

"What's the reason you won't sign it, sir?" returned the Coroner.

"Because, sir, you have not put in the amount that each of us will be taxed to defray the funeral expenses," was the reply.

The poor fishermen were thunder-struck. A sudden "change came o'er the spirit of their dream." To lose their fishing trip, when the breeze and tide was favorable, was bad enough, but the idea of being taxed to pay the burial expenses of a foreigner, was to their minds outrageous.

The Coroner looked at my friend, and his countenance portrayed feelings of mingled pity and contempt, at this exposition of his gross ignorance. He replied, in a harsh tone:

"We hain't got nothing to do with burying the man."

"Why not?" rejoined his tormentor. "I heard you say a short time since that he had no friends or relatives in this country, nor any property; and if you've made up your mind to let the poor fellow lay there and rot, I'll have nothing more to do with this jury, but go and report to the 'State's Attorney' the whole matter. I'm willing to do my part, and if any of the jury are poor, and can't afford to pay, I'm willing to subscribe and pay more than my share. If there is anything I detest on earth, it is a man who will sneak out in a case of this kind. But you won't find, sir, anything sneaking in my disposition.

"I tell you, sir, that I have been very much inconvenienced by being obliged to serve on this jury. I had an appointment to meet two ladies this evening, one at seven, and the other at eight o'clock. But, sir, I did not beg off, and say I could not serve. I sir, was willing to forego the pleasure of worshipping at the shrine of Venus this evening, and remain here to deliberate on this very *grave subject.*"

My friend spoke so rapidly that the bewildered Coroner was unable to get in a word edgewise; but when he ceased, the Coroner replied:

"I see, sir, that you do not understand the matter at all. If the man has no friends to bury him, it will be done at the expense of the State. We don't come here to be taxed, only to find out how the man come to die, and we get pay for our services from the State."

"O! Ah!! That sets the matter in a very different light. Why didn't you say so before, and then we should all have understood it. But it's all right, now, let's proceed with the examination," replied the tormentor.

"Have you not talked with the witnesses?" asked the Coroner.

"I talked with them? why, bless you, I have not been introduced to one of them, yet," was the rejoinder.

"What do you wish to have done?" asked the Coroner, who appeared to be much perplexed, and it was evident he did not know what to do himself.

"I would have the witnesses called up to testify," was the answer.

One of the laborers who had been at work with the man, and was with him at the time of his decease, happened to be in the room at the time, but the other witnesses had all left, and there was no one of the party who knew where to find them. My friend arose from his seat, and said:

"*Mr. Coroner and Gentlemen*:—It will be impossible for me to agree with you on a verdict, in the case of this deceased "Exile from Erin," unless I have satisfactory proofs that the poor unfortunate 'cum to die by drinking too much cold water with ice in it.' Our worthy Coroner seems inclined to put this thing through rather too fast. All of you appear to be satisfied that the death was caused by drinking too much 'cold water with ice in it;' but *I* am not satisfied. There lays a poor 'Hibernian,' stretched in 'Death's cold arms,' and all of us must sooner or later submit to the embraces of the grim tyrant. According to the Coroner's statement, he, a short time ago left that beautiful island where the oppressor's yoke bears heavily upon the necks of its oppressed inhabitants. Perchance he left behind him a kind and affectionate wife, who is now a widow, and doting children, who are now orphans. He came to seek a home in the land of the free, where the ample folds of the banner bearing its stars and stripes, would protect him. Perhaps even now, while we are sitting in solemn conclave, that wife may be perusing the first letter that she has received since his arrival in this country, and shedding tears of joy and gratitude, as she learns that he has obtained a situation to labor, and fancying that the time is not far distant when he will remit her money sufficient to pay her passage, and that of her little ones, across the dark, deep, foaming ocean."

Here, the Coroner, who appeared somewhat affected, informed the speaker that the deceased was a single man.

"That matters not," continued the orator; "if, instead of this poor Irishman, some wealthy 'nabob' had been found dead by the road-side, or in a field, the jury of inquest would have been far different from this.

Priests, lawyers and physicians, would have been called in, and instead of the investigation of an hour, their examinations and deliberations would have lasted two or three days. And now, gentlemen, without farther circumlocution, as the witnesses are not to be found, and as I have yet to learn whether this man came to an untimely end in a fit of apoplexy, or by some wound received in a fracas with one or more of his fellow workmen, or whether he did absolutely 'cum to die by drinking too much cold water with ice in it,' I move that we now adjourn until eleven o'clock to-morrow forenoon, and the Coroner be instructed to summon two skilful surgeons, to hold a post-mortem examination, and report to this jury as soon as practical."

In resuming his seat, he added:

"They may get through their examination so that we shall be able to agree upon a verdict to-morrow night; but it may keep us three or four days."

The Coroner found that he had "caught a Tartar;" his arrogant pomposity vanished, and he made no reply, but rising from his chair, he beckoned to my friend, who followed him into a small side room. He then begged that a verdict might be rendered that night, and promised to do anything and everything that was required, if my friend would withdraw his motion, and not insist on having a post-mortem examination held. Finally it was agreed upon between them, that the Coroner should find two of the witnesses, and have them properly sworn and examined, and in the interim a bottle of good brandy was to be procured for the especial use of the Coroner and jurors.

The brandy was brought in, and soon disposed of, and the witnesses were not long detained. The verdict was signed, and the Coroner departed, with the documents in his pocket, apparently well pleased to get out of the muss as easily as he had.

After his departure my friend informed the fishermen jurors that if they had suffered any pecuniary loss by their detention, the State would pay them, and it was the duty of the Coroner to collect it. He further informed them that it would be for their interest to follow up the Coroner, as soon as they returned from their voyage, and not allow him to appropriate their money to his own use. They profited by this advice, and never was an animal of the feline race more worried, annoyed and tormented by a terrier dog than the aforesaid Coroner was by his five fishermen jurors. The probability is, that if he ever again was called to sit upon the body of a defunct Irishman, he was extremely careful in the selection of his jurymen.

I regret to say that there are persons in the community who appear to take much pleasure in annoying the Coroners, and leading them astray. If a man tumbles into the dock, and is rescued without the slightest injury, these people will inform the Coroner that the man is dead, or nearly dead, and then laugh heartily to see him hasten with all convenient speed to the designated scene of action. I have sometimes thought that people who were guilty of thus deceiving these pious and amiable men should be punished. Some legal enactment should be passed by our Legislatures which would reach such cases.

We will now turn our attention to another class of public functionaries, who have for a few years past increased very rapidly, and now they have become more numerous than were the frogs in Egypt, in the days of old Pharaoh. I allude to JUSTICES OF THE PEACE.

In former times it was considered an honor to hold a Justice of the Peace commission; but now every brawling politician can obtain one of these commissions, whenever the party to which he belongs happens to be in the ascendancy. I do not, however, believe the reports which have been credited by some, that for a few years past, Justices' commissions have been sold and peddled out for twelve or fifteen dollars apiece. One reason for my disbelief in this rumor is that many of those who have received commissions could not afford to pay for them, and others who *could* afford to pay that price, would not, because they never could be convinced that they would ultimately receive *quid-pro-quo* for the money thus invested. Probably not one person out of five who have received such commissions, know anything more of the duties pertaining to the office, than the younker, ten years of age, who creeps unwillingly to school. It is, however, absolutely necessary for the aspiring politician and office.seeker to obtain a Justice's commission, because that is a stepping-stone to something higher.

In country towns and villages, Justices of the Peace are called to set in judgment upon offenders of the law, and examine cases, in the same manner; holding the same power and authority as the Justices of the Police, and Recorders' courts. They make strange work of this sometimes. It takes them a long time to get the "hang of the school-house;" consequently, when a case is brought before them (I should say some of them) for examination, and the accused happens to obtain the services of a cunning pettifogger to appear as his counsel, the country Justice is often troubled and distressed. He will examine the Statute Book, and if he cannot fully comprehend the case, he will "run for luck," and either fine or commit the accused, or discharge the party at once.

In a town not forty miles from Boston, there is a Justice of the Peace, who, when he was fifteen years of age could not spell his name correctly, and on one occasion, when asked whether he was a native of North or South America, replied: "I ain't neither; I was born in our house, close down to the red bridge, on Squnacook River."

It may be well to add that this man's father's house was within one mile of the village school, and that he had attended it regularly, two or three months in the year, for eight years at least.

The first trial that was ever held, where this learned functionary presided, was in a case where a sailor, who had just arrived from a long voyage, was brought before him for riotous and disorderly conduct. It appeared that Jack was on a journey to visit some relatives, but getting too much grog aboard, the stage-driver concluded to leave him in the town where our learned Justice resided, and thus give him an opportunity to sleep off the effects of the liquor. The tavern landlord, finding that Jack was inclined to break up his crockery and furniture, called for the town constable, and after considerable trouble Jack was placed in durance.

The next morning, our Justice, who had been sent for, repaired to the sitting-room of the tavern, to sit in judgment on this important case. After considerable trouble and delay, a complaint was drawn up and read to the prisoner. The sailor, who had not the slightest recollection of anything that had occurred the night previous, supposed that he was on trial for being engaged in a melee in the city, just after having left his ship; and when asked whether he was guilty or not, replied:

"Your Honor, just hear my story, and then you can judge for yourself.

"Well, you see, your Honor, when I cum up from board ship, I was cruising through one of the streets just below here, when I espied a trig looking little craft running before the wind, under bare poles, followed by that old droger, (pointing to the constable,) trying to get his grappling irons aboard of her. I tacked about, and followed close in their wake; presently I cum up alongside. Avast heaving, says I. Well, your Honor, I squared my yards, and gave the lubberly pirate one in the larboard blinker, and then took him below, between wind and water, and that troubled his bread-basket a little, so that he had to strike his colors. Why, your Honor, the little sail he was in chase of, was the trimmest little craft you ever saw in petticoats, and if she hadn't run up a signal of distress, I shouldn't bore down on the lubberly devil. But, your Honor, I guess I didn't hurt him much, for you can see his figure-head and side-lights ain't damaged much, are they, your Honor?"

The Justice, who had sat with open eyes and mouth, listening to Jack's harangue, without comprehending anything he had said, turned to the constable, and asked him if he knew what it all meant?

"Oh! he knows well enough, your Honor," cried Jack. "He won't deny chasing the gal down street, last night; and because I gave him a broadside that made him heave-to, you've got me up here, and are going to make me pay damages, I suppose. But let me ketch the lubber adrift some day, and I'll show him the difference between a hand-saw and marlin-spike."

The constable averred that he believed the man was insane—that he had chased no girl the night previous, and didn't know what the fellow meant—that he had arrested him the night before, for noisy and riotous conduct, and brought him before the Court.

Before the trial had proceeded farther, the Justice was called out by a man who wanted to swap horses with him, and he adjourned the court for a short time, leaving the prisoner in charge of the constable.

When the Justice returned, neither officer or prisoner could be found. The latter, however, was subsequently discovered in one of the stable horse-stalls, fast asleep.

It appears that after the Justice had retired, the officer convinced Jack that he was laboring under a great mistake, with regard to his identity. Jack, in return, had apologized, and gone with the officer into the barroom, where he had, as the Frenchmen say, treated him "three, four, several times," and when the constable became a little oblivious, the sailor stepped out, and never returned to have his examination finished.

When witnesses are upon the stand at an examination where a country Justice presides, they will (if they are his townsmen, and intimately acquainted with him,) make themselves very familiar, and perfectly at home, while giving in their testimony.

A country bumpkin, after having been sworn, will sometimes commence after this wise :

"Neow Squire, I'm going to tell you all I know about this matter, and darn'd quick, too. You recollect the day that your brother Sam bought that yoke of brindled cattle ? you know you said one of 'em was too free for 'tother, and so he was. Well, you see, I was going by old Kezar's house, arter that, 'cause I'd just been talking with Captain John ; he's a Justice of Peace too, I 'spose, but I don-no whether he is or not; and I see old Kezar talking with that chap there, (the witness will point to the defendant) and I kinder mistrusted that old Kezar was trying to sell him his trundle-bed mare, 'cause she's an ugly critter, an' only two or three days afore that, when he went into the barn, and never said a word to her, she up and kicked him right on his hand. So thinks I, I'll just go up and hear what they're talkin about ; but jest as quick as I cum up they stopped a talkin. So I went along, 'cause you see I was going up to Aunt Lucinda's, and I kinder thought that that chap looked jest like the old Methodist parson that stole the oats out of Col. Hoar's stable ; you recollect him, Squire, 'cause you fined him ten dollars and costs, or go to Concord Jail a month. I recollect it jest as well as though it warn't only yesterday. There was a terrible revival of religion here 'bout that time, you know, Squire. Joe Graves he got converted, but didn't do him much good, 'cause he backslid arterwards. Well, as I was telling you, I went up and told Aunt Lucinda how I see that chap talking with old Kezar, and I guessed he was trying to buy the mare, and if he did, he'd get cheated; but when I come to tell her how he looked jest like the old Methodist parson, she turned round and said: Well, I declare, there is so many wolves round here in sheep's clothing, that it's dangerous being safe. Now that's all I know 'bout the scrape, Squire, but jest as soon as I'd heard you'd got him up here to be tried, I thought I'd cum up and tell you what I knew 'bout it, cause father said it was my duty to.

"What's the fellow been doing, Squire? I don-no as I exactly understand what you're trying him for."

The Justice will inform the witness that the man has been put on trial for stealing a watch. The witness, all astonished, will exclaim:

"Good Lord! you don't say so! Bill Tarbell told me that it was for cheating John Gowen, the horse-jockey; but I'll go out and see 'bout that, Squire, and find out all 'bout it."

I know the reader will say that this is double distilled nonsense, and that no man who could obtain a Justice's commission would sit and allow any person to hold forth upon the witness-stand in this manner. Be not too fast in drawing your conclusions. Probably that Justice expects to be nominated as a candidate for State Representative, or some other important office, and perhaps that witness may be good for ten or fifteen votes; and to affront him, either in court or out of court, would blast all his future hopes and prospects, and strike a death-blow to all his well-laid schemes and plans. The aspiring Justice, who is looking for a seat in the Assembly Room, and imagines that the time may come when he will be inducted into the halls of Congress, had better have a mill-stone fastened to his neck, and be drowned in the depths of the sea, than to offend one of these little ones.

To substantiate a statement I have already made, that many who receive a Justice's commission do not understand what their rights, powers or duties are, I will relate a transaction which occurred two or three years ago, in the office of an attorney, who was himself a Justice of the Peace.

An important trial was near at hand, and one of the most important witnesses was obliged to leave this section of the country before the trial came on. By, and with the consent of all parties, his deposition was taken. On the morning of his departure, he went into the attorney's office, to affix his signature to the deposition, and take the required oath. The attorney was not present, and the gentleman requested the clerk to go out and find a Justice, who would come in and officiate for the nonce.

While he was yet speaking, a rough, sturdy old fellow came into the office, and inquired for the Squire.

"He is not in," said the clerk; "but you have come very opportunate. This gentleman wishes to leave in the next train of cars, but before he goes, he must swear to this affidavit; and you, being a Justice of the Peace, will do as well as Squire G—— himself."

"Wa'll, I 'spose I could," replied the countryman, "but I don't know nothin' about the matter, and I guess you'd better wait 'till the Squire comes in; there may be some mistake about it."

The clerk assured the timid Justice that there could be no possibility of a mistake, the papers having been carefully examined by the gentleman, who was ready to affix his signature to them.

The Justice took the documents, turned them over and over, as though he was carefully examining them, then holding them out at arm's length, he requested the gentleman to raise up his right hand.

"Neow," said he, "I don-no much abeout this, but I 'spose it's all right. *Neow you solemnly swear that all you've rit deown on this ere paper is true, by God!*"

The gentleman signed the document, and departed, not much pleased (he being a religious man) with this new, curious, and unique, style of administering, or taking an oath.

A country Justice in New Hampshire, who had done the State (the democratic party, I mean,) some service, was advised (after Franklin Pierce had been elected President,) to go to Washington, and apply personally to him for a lucrative office. His friends assured him that there was no doubt of his obtaining any office he wished, as Mr. Pierce had been his counsellor in two or three cases of litigation. Flushed with the idea of success, the gentleman started; but when he arrived at Washington, he found some trouble in getting a private interview with the President. Finally he succeeded, and the President, who instantly recognized him, receiv ed him cordially, without having the idea enter his head that he was an office-seeker with the rest who were continually annoying him; but great was his astonishment and dismay, when his New Hampshire friend exclaimed:

"Well, General, our folks up in New Hampshire advised me to come on here and get an office. Now General, what yer got left?"

"I do not think there is any office that is not filled," replied the President.

"O! then I 'spose you've promised them all out, without thinking of the New Hampshire boys. Can't you give us a collector's berth in New York, Philadelphia or Baltimore?"

"Those appointments are all made," replied the President.

"You don't say so!" was the response. "Then give us a minister's berth to England, France, Ireland, Gibaralter or Newfoundland; I don't care which it is, so long as the pay's any ways decent."

The President informed him that all the appointments had been made, and there was no vacancy to fill.

The Justice rolled the huge cud of tobacco which he had in his mouth from one side to the other, and was at a loss what to say, or how to order his speech. After a few moments deliberation, he asked if there was no vacancy in some country Post-office?

The President told him that he thought there was not.

"Well, General," said he, "it's a little too darn'd bad for me to come clean on here, and not get nothin' at all."

Then eyeing the President from head to foot, he said:

"General, you wear pretty good clothes, don't you? I 'spose you don't wear a suit of clothes more than three or four weeks; now I was a thinkin', as you and I are about of a size, *if you can't give me no office, you might give me one or two suits of your cast off clothes, that you've laid aside, and that would be better than nothin', anyhow.*"

Whether the President acquiesced in this modest request, or otherwise, deponent saith not.

Whenever a man is brought in contact with a country

Justice, a little "blarney," and a large quantity of "soft soap," discreetly used, and carefully laid on, will work wonders. Many a man has managed to work himself out of what is sometimes called an ugly scrape, by wagging an oily tongue; and as the greatest rogues are for the most part very shrewd and cunning men, they well understand how to play the game, when chance or necessity brings them in proximity with these functionaries, not only when they are brought before them for examination, charged with committing some crime, or for the violation of some law, but also at other times, when they are maturing plans to cheat and defraud some of their fellow men, and laying themselves liable to be detected, and brought up to answer before one of these "soft headed noodles."

When the law, which is commonly called the "Maine Liquor Law," was in full operation in the State where it originated, I was passing through a small town near Bangor, (the name of which I have entirely forgotten,) and accidentally meeting two friends, I was prevailed upon to remain with them over night, they promising to accompany me on my journey the next day. After we had finished our dinner, as we sat conversing together at the table, I requested the waiter to bring in a bottle of claret wine. He informed me that they had nothing of the kind in the house, while my friends, after a roar of laughter, assured me that there was not a drop of wine or liquor to be obtained within ten miles of that place.

"But is there no Town Agency, where spirits are lawfully sold ?" I inquired.

I received an affirmative answer, but was told that the Town Agent was a cross-grained old Justice of the Peace, who would not allow one drop of spirits to go out of his house, (where a large quantity was deposited,) unless the applicant first obtained a physician's prescription.

I quietly remarked that I believed I could go to him, and purchase any moderate quantity of wine or spirits that I asked for, provided he had them in his house.

"You can't do it, my dear boy," replied one of my companions, "for we have tried that ourselves."

While we were talking, the landlord came into the room, and one of my friends said in a jocose way :

"This gentleman thinks that he can go to your Town Agent, and purchase wines or liquors, without a physician's prescription.

"I wager ten dollars that he cannot get a drop, unless he uses deception and false representations."

"I will accept that wager," said I, "and will use neither. Bring me a bottle, and let some one come with me, to point out the local habitation of this straight-laced Justice, and I will start at once, and see what I can do."

When I arrived at the house, I put the old brass knocker which was attached to the door, and which had the appearance of having done years of service, into rapid and active motion, to inform the inmates of the dwelling that there was some one without who craved an entrance.

Presently the Justice himself opened the door.

"Your servant, sir," said I. "I understood that you was the Town Agent, authorized by law to sell spirituous liquors, for mechanical and medicinal purposes, and I wish to get a pint of very nice brandy.

The old fellow was remarkable civil, but he briefly informed me that it would be impossible for him to comply with my request, giving sundry reasons for his declining. He however invited me to walk in, and ushered me into a neat sitting-room, where I found a woman of huge proportions, holding in her arms a juvenile specimen of humanity, and regaling the youngster with that nutriment which is so essential to the growth and well-being of infantiles, and which to them is far prefable to that villainous compound of chalk and water, which is sold and used under the name of milk.

I at once perceived that this "mountain of flesh" was the better half—no, two-thirds—(I like to be liberal, and will say three-quarters) of this dogmatic Justice. I saluted the lady, as I laid my hat upon the table, then rushed towards her, and begged the privilege of taking that "Blessed Baby," in my arms, only for a moment.

The fat scion of an illustrious sire screeched louder than a thousand cat-owls, when they give a sacred concert, as its maternal parent handed it over to me, and I passed it back into the arms of its doting mother very quickly; then taking out an orange, which I happened to have in my pocket, I gave it to the ugly little brat, and commenced complimenting the mother on the beauty, precocity, and intellectuality of the child. I could see in it some of the mother's looks, especially in the eyes; but the lower part of the face, the nose, mouth, and chin, was all father. I could recollect what a sore thing it was for me to lose a darling child, about the same age, who looked very much like that, (it would have puzzled me to tell when or how I lost it,) and I envied those happy parents, who had those heaven-sent blessings spared to them.

I applied my white cotton handkerchief to my eyes and nose, (particularly the latter) and signified my intention to depart.

The Justice arose from his big arm-chair, and coming towards me, he asked, in a low tone of voice, how much brandy I wanted?

"A pint will answer my turn," I replied.

"Did you bring a bottle with you?" said he.

I told him I had; and handed him the flask, which

had in all probability been filled and refilled many times with the same medicine that I was in search of.

The bottle was filled, and replaced in my pocket. The Justice only charged what he said was the first cost of the liquor, (which proved to be very good,) and I returned to the hotel, where my two friends and the landlord sat ready to receive me.

Their astonishment was great when I placed the flask upon the table, but still greater when I assured them that I did not inform his Honor for what purpose I wanted the liquid, neither did he ask me a single question respecting it.

It was the vote of the party, at my suggestion, that the landlord should pay for the brandy, and retain the ten dollars, which he acknowledged he had lost, and which honestly, as he asserted, belonged to me.

It has grieved me much to notice, of late years, the disposition which many (I might say nearly all) of the newly appointed Justices of the Peace have shown, to sink the dignity of their honorable titles. There are a few exceptions, I grant, but those are so rare that the fledglings scarcely know where to find a man who has worn the honors with the grace and dignity becoming the office, whom they can look up to as a pattern and example.

There is one, that I know of, in the city of Boston, who never does, under any circumstances, lose sight of, or forget the great weight of responsibility that rests upon him, and the vast importance of informing all those with whom he may come in contact, (especially those who hail from his native country, "ould Ireland,") the necessity of showing due respect to the office, if not to the man.

A Justice of the Peace will walk into a "Bar-room," a theatre, or a political meeting, where some of his friends and acquaintances are congregated, and how is he saluted? Do they raise their hats with respect, as they approach him, extend their hands respectfully to salute him, and assure him they did not expect the honor of his company on that occasion? Not at all! One will cry out: "There comes 'Old Sam'!"--another will say (while slapping the Justice on the back): "He's a jolly old dog, anyhow,"—while another still will exclaim: "I'm devilish glad to see you! How's the old woman getting along, and what's that last sprout of yours'? Is it a 'boy' or a 'gal'?" Now all this must be very annoying to our Justice, and will distress him. But where is his remedy? If he assumes the dignity pertaining to his station, his former friends and companions will cry out: "Oh! he's putting on airs," and they will cut his acquaintance at once. It will be much better for him to lose his commission, than to lose his friends, and as he wishes to retain both, he is obliged to submit.

In my opinion, a man, after he has received a Justice of the Peace commission, should throw aside all frivolity, and claim at once the high standing in society to which he is entitled by virtue of his office. It is not absolutely necessary for him to wear a badge, like a policeman, but he should, like the Hibernian Justice I have spoken of, allow no opportunity to pass where he has the slightest chance to make known to the world that he must and will be respected.

Whenever he sees a free fight, in full tide of successful operation, he should have pluck and courage enough to count himself in as one. But when he sees the chances are against him, and finds that a portion of the brain (of which he has none to spare) is in imminent danger of changing its position, he should have presence of mind enough to cry out: "I'm a Justice of the Peace, and if you strike me, you strike the Commonwealth." But it is not necessary for a Justice of the Peace to make himself known on such occasions, unless he finds that he will receive great bodily harm and injury, and where the odds are greatly against him, for the very good reason, that if he is armed with a good club, and has sufficient courage to rush into a crowd, knock down some fifteen or twenty, and disperse the remainder, he not only saves the State the expense of trials of the parties concerned in the affray, but establishes a name (among the fighting men in particular) of possessing great courage and herculean strength, which are to him indispensable qualifications of office.

As Justices of the Peace are authorized to unite in the holy bonds of wedlock those who prefer their services to those of the priest or minister, it is very necessary for them to keep a sharp lookout for the chances; and on all such occasions they will find it much for their interest to be very liberal in their charges. Many of this class of functionaries do not thoroughly understand this, and often let opportunities pass, which, if taken at the proper time, would give them great notoriety and influence, although such opportunities may not put money in their pockets. Some of them, more shrewd than others, will notify the public of the important fact, after they have received their commissions, by inserting notices in the journals of the day, that they are authorized, by the power in them vested, to perform the marriage ceremony, and they will cordially invite those who wish to enter into this ancient and time-honored co-partnership, to call upon them at their offices, where the business will be finished up with neatness and dispatch.

But there is one thing which these newly appointed Justices (who advertise for business entirely) overlook when they solicit patronage, and that is, their prices and charges, which they want and expect for their services. I think an advertisement something after this style would be of great advantage to many of them, while they are seeking a sustenance in this selfish and mercenary world :

"Peleg Tieumquick, having been duly appointed a Justice of the Peace, in and for the State of ———, offers his services to all who may stand in need of them, (irrespective of party or political opinions,) to administer oaths, perform marriage ceremonies, prosecute those who are guilty of inflicting punishment upon animals, &c., &c. Charges very moderate, viz. :

For performing the marriage ceremony, 31 cts.

For administering an oath, 15 cts.

Advice gratis. Those from the country usually preferred ; and all business letters strictly confidential ! Competition defied ! !"

An advertisement of this kind could not fail to draw crowds of people to the office of an aspiring Justice, provided all our Justices did not adopt the same plan, at one and the same time. In that case, newspaper publishers would be obliged to enlarge the size of their sheets, and have no room left for editorials or items.

Justices of the Peace should belong to one or more churches ; and as it is impossible for a man to have too much of a good thing, and as I never yet saw a Justice of the Peace who was possessed of too much piety or good-will towards his fellow-men, perhaps our Legislatures could not do better than to enact a law which would oblige every Justice of the Peace to attend church regularly, every Sabbath-day, allowing them the same privilege that physicians have, of employing a person to stand in the porch, to rush in during divine service, and call them out, so that the congregation may be advised of the fact (or what they would have the world believe to be a fact,) that outside suffering humanity demands their services.

It may not be absolutely necessary for a Justice of the Peace to be a meddling, inquisitive man, but he should, as far as practicable, keep himself well informed respecting the movements, actions, customs and habits, of his immediate neighbors and others with whom he may come in contact, so that whenever he is invited to a party, or makes one himself, he can edify and instruct the company, by laying before them a full *expose* of such and such persons' domestic affairs, and especially those who make a great outside show, to make, if possible, the world believe that they are in good circumstances, when they are not. Such people should be looked after, and it is the business only of old maids and "fogy" Justices to attend to them.

But the duties of a Justice of the Peace are so multifarious, that it is impossible for me to note all of them, and I will close this chapter.

JACOB C. TALLANT.

(See Page 107.)

CHAPTER IX.

Juries and Jurors—The Crooked Sticks who are sometimes drawn as Jurors—Excuses made to get excused—The Juror who obtained his brandy in an unlawful manner—Courts in the Western Settlements—An extensive Jury Room—Novel way of obtaining a verdict—Inoperative laws passed to suppress Swindling and Fraud—The plan adopted by many to cheat Wholesale Merchants—The injurious effects of the Swindler upon the honest man—Money obtained by gambling not considered swindling—Glance at the Lawyers in the Senate Chambers and Houses of Assembly—Ignorance of voters—Grog Shops in the city of Boston—The Rifle, Revolver, Bowie-knife, &c.

I will now turn the attention of the reader to court juries and jurymen. Probably there is no one thing that a business man, whether he be merchant or mechanic, trader, broker or banker, dreads more, (excepting death or a protested note) than being drawn as a juror. Many men who are thus drawn, resort to the most curious devices to get excused from serving in that capacity. Some are taken suddenly and violently sick, others have sickness in their families, or have a near relative lying at the point of death, and they cannot serve;

others when they are impanneled as jurors in the criminal courts, will when the first case comes up for trial, (if it is an important one) declare that they have formed and expressed an opinion in the case pending, and therefore, incompetent to give an unbiased verdict; while another will by grimmaces and vindictive looks, cause the prisioner at the bar to challenge him peremptorily. These and various other stratagems are resorted to by jurors who do not wish to serve the Commonwealth to their own detriment.

Sometimes a juror is impanneled who will serve during the whole term, and make himself as obnoxious as possible, not only to his brother jurors, but also to the court. These "crooked sticks" appear to take delight in blocking the wheels of the Car of Justice. If the evidence in a case which has been tried, is as clear as the rays of the sun, they cannot or will not see it. They are dissatisfied with the ruling of the Judge. They think that the testimony of such and such a witness should be thrown out, because the witness swore too much, or too little, or perhaps the juryman will sit in dogged silence, without giving the whys or the wherefors of his refusal to acquiesce in a verdict with his compeers.

I have seen cases where one juryman would sit after the eleven others had agreed, and with much nonchalance inform them, that rather than to agree with them in their verdict, he would remain in the jury-room until the flies had carried off his carcass through the key-hole of the door. When asked if he wanted any farther instruction from the Judge, respecting any points of law? He replied, "No! all the Judges that ever lived since the days of old Moses, would not alter my mind, or change my opinion!"

The scenes sometimes enacted in a jury-room are ludicrous, and if they were brought before the eyes of the world, it would not tend to exalt the participants in the estimation of the community.

Before the temperance reformation, when jurors were confined for a long time, and were unable to agree upon a verdict, they were allowed a little stimulant for their stomach's sake, and it has often been found that the "Rosy God" has been more effectual in bringing a refractory juror into the traces, than all the attornies arguments, or Judges charges, that were ever concocted or delivered.

Shakespeare was not partial to Judges. He says, "some of them would rather hang the guiltless, than eat their mutton cold." We have some of that class even in our day, among jurors as well as Judges.

Jurors will sometimes resort to expedients and obtain a drop of the "crature comfort," when they have been long confined in a jury-room, and could see no possible chance for an agreement upon a verdict. Many times, and often when their food has been taken to them, some peculiarly marked loaf of bread, or nicely roasted chiken, has been known to contain a small mysterious looking bottle. How it came there—what its contents were, or for what purpose it was to be used, I leave the reader to judge.

On one occasion, (a very sultry day in July,) a jury had been confined to their room for several hours. From their windows the jurymen could look directly into the saloon of a celebrated restorant, where their more fortunate fellow citizens, who were not confined under lock and key, were apparently enjoying themselves by imbibing "Brandy Smashers, Sherry Coblers, Mint Julips' and other cooling beverages.

One of the jurymen wrote a note, fastened a small weight to it, and as one of his friends came out of the aforesaid restorant, he threw out the note, which landed directly at the feet of the gentleman below. He picked it up, read it, re-entèred the restorant and presently appeared with a small package wraped in a newspaper. A small cord or twine was lowered from the window of the jury-room to which the mysterious package was quickly attached, and it was drawn up to the window carefully, but rapidly. Upon the arrival of this wonderful and welcome visitor, every juryman was anxious to be informed of its contents, and when it was exposed to view, the words, "Old Otard" was seen in gilded letters on the outside, many a lip stood ready to give it a smack. But few minutes elapsed ere the contents of the magic bottle had entirely disappeared.

Great was the rejoicing among some eight or nine of the jurymen, who boldly declared they were refreshed both in body and soul, although they could not agree upon a verdict, they were unanimous in the opinion that "Mr. Otard" was a good and soul-consoling man. But the bitter sometimes follows the sweet. The foreman of the jury, a straight faced, psalm-singing old curmudgeon, was shocked and horrified at such a procedure. He raised his hands, and with crocodile tears in his eyes, informed the juryman who introduced this contraband visitor, that he considered it his solemn and bounden duty to inform the court of this diabolical arrangement, and have the transgressor brought to condign punishment.

The next morning when the court came in, our valiant hero in the cause of temperance, laid the facts before the Judge, and our juror of the "string and bottle" was arraigned to answer for the misdemeanor.

He pleaded guilty, but in extenuation of the awful crime, stated that he was not aware that he was committing an overt act, that he was, slightly troubled with dyspepsy and dysentry, that he had during the afternoon, drank large quantities of ice-water, that the dinner sent to the jury on that day, consisted of tough roast goose and apple-dumpling, which lay on his stomach like granite boulders, and in his opinion no other medicine could have reached his case.

The Judge reprimanded him, and discharged him from farther duty, for which our juryman expressed his sincere and heartfelt thanks.

In new settlements in the Middle and Western States, where log-houses containing but one room are used for the holding of courts, the juries when they repair for consultation, generally start for some retired spot in the woods, where they can squat down or repose under the shady branches of some lofty oak. There with a huge jug of whiskey beside them, they will discuss the merits and demerits of the case; and when they cannot agree upon a verdict, they will decide by drawing lots, or pitching coppers, to see who shall "give in first." Their consultations do not generally last long, although there is less formality, there is more justice usually rendered in those Courts, than we find in the tribunals of the Northern and Eastern States.

In almost every State in the Union, laws have been enacted with a view to prevent fraud and swindling—to punish people of every grade and profession who obtain goods, chattles, and other valuables by false pretenses.

No penal law ever enacted, has been more carefully considered and thoroughly analyzed than this, by all our law-givers in every section of the country; but I make bold to say, that there is not a law upon the Statute Books that operates so unequally.

Let us glance at the law. A cool calculating villian who is not worth one dollar, and perhaps owes for the very clothes he wears upon his back, will by the aid of two or three accomplices, go into the ware-house of the merchant, and with sanctified face and oily tongue—with cheek, brass and impudence, represent himself worth fifty or sixty thousand dollars. His accomplices are sojourning at the most fashionable hotels, where they can be found at business hours; but after nightfall if you would see them look for them in some gambling saloon. The swindler carries in his gilded pocket-book, letters of recommendation, purporting to be given by well known and distinguished gentlemen; his dress is scrupulously neat, mock brilliant studs adorn his shirt-bosom, a massive galvanized watch and chain are conspicuous, as he takes much pains to display them, while two or three real, or imitation diamond rings adorn his fingers.

The merchant is delighted with his customer, and the customer equally well pleased with his dupe.

Shortly afterwards the merchant finds he has been

swindled, and causes his *quasi* friend to be arrested. He is brought to trial. The accomplices swear that they believe the defendant to be an honest and fair dealing man. The Court decides according to law and evidence. The defendant is acquitted, and as he departs snaps his fingers in the face of the victimised merchant.

Let us look at another case.

A young man of good moral character commences business with a few thousand dollars, success attends him, business is good, he has large profits and wealthy customers (as he imagines.) He is flattered by all, and believes that he is on the high road to fortune, he thinks himself worth five times as much as he really is; he boldly asserts that he is worth twenty thousand dollars, when in reality he is not worth one fifth of that amount. (He also purchases of the same merchant who has been swindled by a practical villian.) The value of the goods decrease fifty per cent. while on his hands. Notes held by him which he considered good, prove to be valueless. Creditors press in upon him, and he finds his only recourse is to wind up his affairs, distribute equally among the creditors his effects, and commence the world anew.

Our merchant who has been so egregiously swindled by the fashionable "Jerrimy Diddler" is not willing to receive twenty or thirty cents on the dollar. No! He had rather put swindler No. 2 (as he calls him) through a course of law. He will have him indicted for obtaining goods under false pretenses. Witnesses stand ready to swear that the debtor has openly proclaimed himself worth twenty-five thousand dollars (more or less) when he made extensive purchases, but only a small part of that can be found. They will swear that they have reason to believe, and do believe, that the debtor has secreted or covered his property for the purpose of defrauding his creditors. If the debtor has no wealthy friend to stand by him in this emergency, he is convicted and doomed to a felons cell, "The law decrees it, and the Judge awards it."

Reader, look at both pictures as I have drawn them, and tell me if it is not really and truly so. Do not the innocent often suffer for the sins of the guilty, not only in such cases as I have cited, but in others of a different grade?

When the Hon. George H. Campbell was elected Judge of Calveras Co., California, in the year 1849, one of the first cases that came before him for adjudication, was that of a green-horn who wished to obtain a warrant for the arrest of a man, whom he averred, had defrauded him out of every dollar he possessed by false pretenses.

Perhaps I cannot do better than to lay before the

reader the report of a case which was brought before the Police Court of Buffalo a short time ago, which is synonymous with that of Judge Campbell's. I am not inclined however, to believe that Judge C. was quite so thoroughly versed in the game of chance played with cards, as the Buffalo Police Court Magistrate.

I will narrate the scene as related to me by a court reporter.

An elderly man fashionably dressed was seen hanging around the bench of the court. After some hesitation, he walked up to the magistrate, saying:

"Judge, I want a warrant."

"Well," said the Justice, "what do you want the warrant for?"

"False pretenses your honor."

"Who is the individual you wish to arrest?"

"It is Jem Sikes. You see he went and—"

"Now, just stop," said the Justice, "and answer my questions. What did Jem Sikes do."

"Well, you see, squire, he come the false pretenses ever me. Just as I was going up to roost last night I met Jem, and says he to me, 'just come into my room and we'll have a game of *bluff*.' "

"Don-no nothing about it says I. 'Nor I, neither, says he, 'but I'll show you how it is done.' Then you see, squire, I went in, and—"

"What did you do then," asked the Justice, who appeared somewhat interested in the case.

"Well squire, Jem showed me how they bet on 'pars' and them wot had the most 'pars' took the 'pile' wot was up. So you see, squire, I won two or three pots, and then Jem won a small pot."

"Well," said the Justice, "go on."

"Then, Jem he delt, and I swear if there warn't three queens in my hand; and says I, I'll bet ten dollars on two pars; then says Jem, 'I'll just see that, and go you ten dollars better.'"

"Well, and what then," said the Justice.

"Well, Jem looked at his hand, and laughing said; 'Can you beat four kings?' And that skeart me, 'cause I know'd three queens could'nt beat four kings. So I did'nt bet, and Jem snaked down the pile. So you see, squire, I want a warrant for him, on false pretenses."

"You can't have it." shouted the Justice. "On what ground do you claim it."

"Well, you see, Jem asked me if I could beat four kings, and I know'd three queens—"

"On what grounds do you claim it," asked the Justice. "You lost your money, did'nt you?"

"Yes, but you see, I helt three queens, and Jem asked me if I could beat four kings, and I know'd well enough that three queens would'nt beat four kings; so I throw'd up my hand, and he snaked down the pile. He never had four kings at all. Give us a warrant, won't you, Squire?"

"What did Jem hold," asked the Justice.

"He never helt nothing at all, onny two *leetle par.*"

The complainant was ordered to leave the court-room, and he started off execrating the law that did not allow a man to seize the pile when he helt three queens, and allowed another chap to rake him down when he "did'nt hold *nothing onny two leetle par.*"

This case, with kindred others, equally ridiculous, demonstrate the fact that there are hundreds of men, I might say thousands, who have but an indefinite idea of the laws pertaining to fraud. It is not in the power of man to enact laws which will operate equally when brought to bear upon the just and the unjust in business transactions, unless the "credit system" is entirely abolished. In my humble opinion every man who gives his friend or neighbor credit, should, Andrew Jackson like, "take the responsibility." If I loan money to another there is no coercion. If I contract with a man, friend or stranger, and deliver over to him an amount of goods without having first received *quid pro quo*, should I not do it at my own risk? After they are bargained for and delivered to the purchaser, do they not become his property? Are there not laws now extant to protect every man, to hold, defend and enjoy all that rightfully belongs to him? Most certainly there is! Why then were laws enacted to punish a man by confining him in a prison, when he had committed no criminal or overt act? I leave the reader to answer this question. If he cannot readily do it, I would ask him to visit the Senate Chambers and Houses of Assembly, where the Representatives of the people meet to enact laws. Go there and see your Scrub Lawyers—braying asses, whose ears cannot be disguised, chosen by those who pride themselves upon their liberties, their republican institutions and laws. Go watch and see who and what these men are, who are appointed on committees of the judiciary, &c. Are not two-thirds of them lawyers? Is there a man living, possessed of what is called common sense, who would for a moment suppose that these men exert themselves to pass laws which would benefit others to the detriment of themselves, and put money in a poor man's pocket to their own loss? Do the majority of those elected to frame laws (however well they may be paid from a treasury overrunning with the monies collected in the form of taxes from the laborer, mechanic, and trader,) cooly and calmly throw self-interest aside, and legislate for the benefit of their constituents.

I am not writing as a partisan! Let those dabble in politics who will; but when I see men who are incompetent to hold a plough, drive a team, wield an axe, or engage in any occupation which will benefit mankind, sent up to our Council Chambers to enact laws, two thirds of which are designed to make the rich, richer, and the poor, poorer. I do not wonder that legislation increases day by day, and year by year? Are not the laws enacted by our fathers wise enough, stringent enough, and good enough for their children? If the spirits of departed statesmen ever revisit the glimpes of the moon, and watch the doings of our law-givers, and law-dispensers of the present day, every summer's evening breeze, and the howling winds of winter, through which their spirits moved, would tell us in mournful whispers in the one, and trumpet-tongued in the other, that "Ichabod" should be written on every wall.

There are at the present time, laws upon the Statute Books of every Northern and Eastern State which remain as dead letters. In proof of this, I would refer the reader to the Statute Books of Massachusetts alone. New laws are yearly enacted; but, there are many that become obsolete, and never have been repealed. I would seriously ask, why is this? Is it, or is it not, for the benefit of those who are chosen blindly, by the people, who enact laws, so fixed and so framed that not one man in a thousand can understand or comprehend them?

Why is it that the city of Boston (not to speak of other cities, and suburban towns) support scores of self-styled attornies, who are too lazy to work at any reputable calling, whereby they might obtain an honest living? It must follow as a matter of course that those who have the power in their hands to enact laws, will, if possible, frame them to suit not only their own views, but their own interests.

Who is benefited by the constant changing of the laws, in this or any other country? Take Massachusetts, and look at the resolves passed, and Statutes enacted for the past five years. Would not the inhabitants of the State, the middling and poorer classes especially, be better off if the last five Legislatures had never convened? What laws have they enacted which have, or will benefit the poor man? Does the "Lien Law" do it? Find me one journeyman mechanic who has been benefited by that law, and I will find you ten who have attempted to avail themselves of its supposed advantages only to lose their money and precious time, to say nothing of the wages honestly due to them; and all for what? Simply to fee the very men, mostly attornies, who devised and enacted the law.

Does the law abolishing imprisonment for debt in Massachusetts, benefit the poor man as it now stands upon our Statute Books? Let us see.

The veriest rogue that ever escaped the hangmans halter, can go before a Justice and swear any honest man (who happens to be so unlucky as to have any dealings with him) into a prison cell, from which he cannot be released until lawyers, costs, and other contingent expenses are paid.

"I thank heaven, my father and myself," that I have never yet had the slightest practical experience in either of the laws I have alluded to.

Would it not be well for those who spend their time and money in electioneering for candidates who solicit their sufferage, not one out of ten know or care what their constituents really need; instead of huzzaing, shouting, and traversing the streets by daylight and at nightfall, to quietly set down, consider, and investigate the qualifications of those men who aspire to fill the offices of Assemblymen, Representatives, and Senators? Would not the money expended in torchlight processions, mass meetings, caucuses, &c., benefit the middling classes of our community if expended in another way? Does not the laborer, when he leaves his cheeerful fireside and goes forth to join with his fellow laborers after a hard days toil, electioneering for men to fill offices of trust and emolument, without the slightest knowledge of the capabilities, or honesty of those for whom he is shouting, and expending his money, injure himself and family, without receiving any benefit thereby?

Are there not men enough whose honesty and integrity have been tried, and are well known, who would if selected, and elected, go into the Senate Chambers, and with an eye single to the interest of their constituents, legislate for the good of the whole community, without fear or favor? Certainly there is! No reasonable, well informed man doubts it.

Such men are not partisans, they never crawl and fawn to seek office, and therefore are seldom sent to the Capitol to enact laws.

Let those who complain of the laws as they now exist, ask themselves why they are so framed. Under the old license laws enacted to regulate the sale of intoxicating liquors, there was not one half as much drunkenness and rioting, with other crimes which follow close in their wake, as there is at the present time. Of course, I allude to our large towns and cities. If the reader doubts this, let him examine our court reports and statistics, and he will find that I am correct.

Look at the fourteen hundred grog-shops in the city of Boston, not one of which pay a single dollar into the city, county, or state treasury in the form of license fees. More than eleven hundred irresponsible men and women, are allowed to trafic openly and boldly in spirituous liquors in that city, and the major part of those liquors are so execrable and vile, that if used to bathe a crippled mastiff, would seriously injure the animal, if they did not cause instant death.

I make bold to assert, that in every State where the law-makers have been tinkering, altering, enacting, and repealing laws, for the suppression of the sale of intoxicating liquors, they have not only injured the cause of temperance, but they have expended more of the public money in this experimental legislation from year to year, than all the expenses combined, paid for the support of paupers.

When all the present existing sumptuary laws enacted to suppress the sale and use of spirituous liquors are erased from the Statute Books, and the old stringent license laws made and executed by our fathers are replaced in their stead, and rigidly enforced; then, and not till then, will the glorious cause of temperance prosper. Rum-holes and dens of vice will be broken up, and the business in our criminal courts greatly diminished.

If I am correct in these premises; as old Judge F— said on one occasion, when he was reviewing a case which was tried before him. "If the court understand *herself*, and *she* thinks *she* does; then she must acknowledge there is some wit in the argument, although she is not ready to admit so much as she otherwise would be glad to, because it is not popular, and might injure herself in the estimation of the *kimmunity.*"

I have given this subject some consideration and carefully watched the operations of coercive laws when the authorities have attempted to execute them, and found that in nine cases out of ten they were unable to do so. I must necessarily be driven to the conclusion that all laws which cannot be enforced, and are allowed to remain a dead letter upon the Statute Book, have a prenicious tendency upon a portion of the community. Surely this matter is worth a passing consideration from those who have an interest in the welfare of our common country.

In new States and Territories, before a government is properly organized, the settlers are for a time their own personal law-makers, and law-dispensers. The rifle, revolver, and bowie-knife, are the arguments they use; but it is a demonstrated fact, that with these people, even-handed justice is meeted out to violators of the common law, in a manner which would put some of our legal tribunals to the blush. Among those people you find no cunning lawyers, standing ready to move for an 'arrest of judgment,' or 'take exceptions to the ruling of the Court,' no court officers eagerly watching for a postponement of a criminal case, by which their fees would be enhanced, and a few extra dollars be added to the pile that already jingles in their pockets; and no superanuated Judge 'full of wise saws, and modern instances,' blocking the wheels of justice. Every man who conducts himself with propriety, claims and receives the protection of his neighbors, while the transgressor seldom escapes speedy and condign punishment.

The laws adopted by these people are not unlike those which were given to the Jewish nation by 'Moses,' they are however, not quite as stringent, but they are as briefly executed. Although I am no advocate for lynch-law, I have seen cases tried, and persons executed under it, fairly, openly, and I think, justly.

In my next chapter I will narrate the scenes of two trials, which took place in California. A Lynch Judge, presiding. I shall give them as related by my Uncle Zeb, who was an eye witness.

CHAPTER X.

Visit to California—Sketch of the Manners and Customs of the Miners—Their Mode of Settling Quarrels—Account of a Miner who shot an Indian—His Arrest and Examination before a Court of Inquiry—Novel and lucid Charge of a Judge—Trial of a Murderer under the Lynch Law—His Condemnation, Sentence, and Speedy Execution—A Curious Favor for a man to ask, who had but Four Minutes to Live—Description of the mode of executing a Parricide in China—The Louisville Murderer—The Negro Pirate — Defaulters and Swindlers — The Shrewd Young Merchant, &c.

"In the year 1850," said Uncle Zeb, "I visited California, with the intention of remaining a few months to examine a portion of the country, and perchance pick up a few rocks, if any fell in my way. So much has already been said and written respecting this "El Dorado of tenderness and *tin*," that it would be superfluous for me to attempt to give any description, either of the country itself, the natives, or the thousands of adventurers who had for three or four years previous been pouring into this promised land.

I made an excursion to the mines, on and above the

American River. At one section of the diggings, I found a small community, consisting of twenty-five or thirty miners, most of them Americans, and two of them were elderly men, with whom I had a slight previous acquaintance. I concluded to remain with them a short time, and try my luck also, with the pickaxe and shovel.

I had not been long with them, before I made the acquaintance of almost every man, and I was forcibly struck with the apparent good order that prevailed, and the kindly feeling which they entertained toward each other.

After the close of each days work, they would repair to their tents, cook, and eat their suppers; they would then light their pipes, (nearly all of them,) and congregate together in small squads, and wile away a few hours, telling stories, discussing politics, singing songs of home, and drinking large potations of brandy, and that, generally good and pure, except the poisonous stuff manufactured in, and shipped from New-York, or some Atlantic cities of New England.

A few isolated individuals would remain alone in their tents, reading some thumb-worn book or newspaper received from home, or perhaps, perusing for the fiftieth time a letter from a betrothed damsel, who urges him to hasten the time, and return to fulfil loves young promises, and make glad the heart which yearns to behold him once more.

Whenever any difference arose between them, or whenever there was an intricate point to settle, one of the gentlemen to whom I have alluded as having previously known, who gloried in the *soubriquet* of Judge, was looked upon as umpire. His decisions were irrevocable, and from them there was no appeal, although his knowledge of law was very limited, and his opinions as sometimes expressed, were ambiguous and indefinite.

For example:—Early one morning one of the miners left his tent, after having prepared his breakfast, without having eaten it, and was absent fifteen or twenty minutes. In the interim an Indian entered the tent, gathered up the tempting flap-jacks, and other delectable morsels, and quietly vamoosed.

When the miner returned and found his breakfast *non est inventus*, he waxed exceeding wroth, and swore by "the living Moses," that he would take summary vengeance upon the thief, if he could discover him.

Presently one of his companions came into the tent, and informed him that he saw an Indian enter, and leave it a short time before; but supposing the occupant was within, he took no particular notice of him; he could, however, point out the direction which the Indian took. The young man seized his rifle and started in pursuit.

The California Indians are quiet and inoffensive, but filthy, indolent, and thievish. Like the "Cyote," they will prowl about in a sneaking way, ready to pilfer anything, whenever they imagine they are not seen; without intellect enough to calculate upon the chances of afterwards being detected. In fact, they appear to be but a trifling grade above the brute creation.

The young miner who had started upon the trail of the Indian, had traveled about a mile and a half, when, in a small ravine he espied the thief, seated upon the grass, devouring the breakfast which had been especially prepared for another.

The miner cooly brought his rifle to his shoulder, and taking a sure and steady aim "pop went the weasle." The Indian with a piercing shriek leaped from the ground, and falling over backwards expired, with a part of the last flap-jack unmasticated in his mouth.

The miner returned to his tent, put by his rifle, substituted half a pint of brandy for his breakfast, and went to his daily labor.

Although our hero, or murderer, (which ever you please to term him) was very popular among his companions, some of them were not well pleased at this procedure. They avered that the crime did not merit such a punishment. while others said that it was absolutely necssary to pop off a few of the theiving devils, when they were detected; and thus, make examples of them, for the safety and protection of their goods and property, which was necessarily exposed, and liable to be pilfered and carried away.

Finally it was agreed amongst them to convene a court, and allow each man, who was disposed, to express his opinion in the case. The opinion, ruling, and decision of the Judge, was of course, to be considered definite, and final.

The court convened. Much was said *pro* and *con*, and after each one had given his views and opinion upon the the merits of the case before them, the Judge arose somewhat perplexed, as he had discovered that the parties were nearly balanced, and differed materially in their opinions. He then proceeded to address them as follows:—

"Gentlemen. I don-no as I shall make myself fully understood in this matter, 'cause there is a great difference of opinion among the gentlemen who compose this court. You have all argued well on both sides. You all talk well enough, and I think you all mean well enough; but there is one *pint* that none of you have touched on at all, and that is this: Whether or not a California "Injun" is a human critter. Now, really, I don-no whether he is or not. Some of you will say he is; but how you going to prove it? Whar's your authority? Can you find it in Washington's Farewell Address, or in his Declaration of Independence? Guess not! Whar do you find it then? When that good old gentleman said, that all men were born free and equal, did he include California Injuns? Of course he did'nt 'cause he did'nt know anything about the nasty critters! So you see, if you aint got no authority, your argument falls.

Then again, on the other hand, those who argue that a California Injun is a human, responsible critter, don't produce any proof, as I see at all. Some of you say that he is, and some of you say that he aint. Now, how do you 'spose I'm goin' to make a decision in a case where I aint got no proof neither way? The stealing of the flap-jacks have been spoken of. This I know makes it a very agrivated case; for I must tell the truth, and say, that my friend, whose case we are investigating, makes the best flap-jacks of any man in these diggings, and if I had'nt been appointed Judge, more'en like as not, I should have stole some of the flap-jacks myself, if I'd got a good chance, 'cause those are about the only things I've seen worth stealing since I've been here among you; but to have a cursed Injun steal *that kind* of flap-jacks, 'its too bad, and no mistake.

And gentlemen, speaking of flap-jacks, brings up another *pint* which I had almost forgotten. When old Dr. Quickenbosh was here in the diggings he told me, that more'en half the sickness among the miners was caused by using too much salaretus in mixing up their flap-jacks. He argued that salaretus should never be put into the human stomach any way, and the only thing it was good for on God's 'arth, is to put into sour cider, when you are goin' to drink it in the morning before breakfast, and then you should always put in a little good brandy to prevent it from discumboberating the internal intestines; and I am inclined to think the old doctor was more than half right.

I hope you gentlemen will bear in mind, that this is a court of inquiry, and not a court of trial, and you all know, that there is a good deal of difference between the one and t'other. I have not yet during the trial seen or heard any evidence, nor the smallest bit of proof, which leads me to believe that our friend the defendant ever shot an *Injun* any way. True; he says, he did, but he or-ter said, he *thought* he did. He says, the Injun stole his breakfast. That's true, nobody doubts that. He says, he followed the Injun with his rifle, and found him squatting in a ravine chawing up the flap-jacks. That's true, nobody doubts that. But mark you; he then says, that he drew up his rifle—banged away—sent a little joker right through him, between his smeller ana bread-basket, firing at a distance of five or six hundred yards! He then goes on to say, that the Injun squealed once, jumped up, and then went over "kerflummux," with the flap-jack in his mouth, and I have no doubt the defendant really believes that he shot the Injun! But gentlemen, everybody is likely to be deceived some time or 'nother. 'Taint three nights ago, I heard the defendant swear he could snuff a candle at sixty yards with his rifle, nine times out of ten.

"And I swear now I can do it, and I'll bet high on it, with anybody," the prisoner said in an audible voice.

The Judge without paying the slightest attention to this remark of the defendant, continued.

"Nobody saw him snuff the candle at sixty yards, gentlemen, and because he thinks he can do it, is no proof he can. Besides, in the case of the Injun, nobody see him shoot him, and there aint no law to convict a man on his own testimony. Now would'nt it be more reasonable to suppose that the Injun, after stealing them flap-jacks, which I dare say, was full of salaretus, went down into the swamp and began to eat 'em, and you know Injuns aint used to eaten salaretus. Might not, I say, them flap-jacks given the Injun gripes, and the gripes you know will make a man squeal awfully, and sometimes throw him into fits, and when he has them fits he will jump up, "flummux" round, throw up his hand, when he sees he aint neither ace, face, nor trump, and keel over as easy as a stuck pig. I don't say this Injun died that way; but I do say he might have died that way, although the defendant says he shot him; and in any other case but this, I should take his word under oath, as quick as I would any other man's, between here and 'Dead-man's Bar.'

"Under all the circumstances, gentlemen, in fulfiling the duties you have put upon me, I honorably discharge the defendant."

The charge and decision of the Judge was received with approbation. Many of them asserted that he had put a new phase upon the whole matter; that he had conducted the trial fairly and equitably; in fact, they looked upon him as "a second Daniel come to judgment."

Let not the reader infer that the miners there assembled, were ignorant and untutored men, far from it. Many of them had been educated in New England schools, and understood the common law much better than many who fill the jury-seats in some of our Southern and Western courts. But the first law of nature, self-preservation, and the necessity of combining together for the protection of their rights and property, together, with the habits and customs formed after months, perhaps years spent in these wild regions, most of the time with no opportunities to mingle with any other society, except their own; naturally causes them to adopt habits, rules, and regulations, which they would throw off at once, if they were placed in a different situation. If a stranger comes among them, and adapts himself to their rules, and conducts himself with what they call propriety, he is kindly received, and welcomed by all. If he is taken sick, some one of them will look after him. If he dies, they will bury him decently, carefully preserve whatever goods and effects he may have, and inform his relations and friends, if any can be found respecting the same.

"Now," continued Uncle Zeb, "I will relate an account of the first and only capital trial and execution I ever witnessed under what is called 'Linch Law.' I was obliged to be a participator in it, as was every one who happened to be present on the occasion. The scene occured at the same place, and the trial was conducted by the same men who were engaged in the trial I have just described.

"A stout muscular well formed man who had been prospecting in the dry diggings, came among us, and pitched his tent near some deserted claims. He was an Englishman by birth, about forty years of age. His appearance was any thing but prepossessing. His sinister eye, which had a restless snaky look, and the preponderance of the animal passions, indicated that he was not possessed of a mild or amiable disposition, while the broken bridge of his nose, and deep cut scars upon his cheeks, plainly shewed that the fist of some powerful pugilist and his face, had often come in close contact. It was evident from the first, that the miners took a great dislike to him, although they always treated him with civility, if not respect.

"Soon after he came among us, he got into an altercation, about some trivial matter, with a young man from the British provinces, who was much esteemed by our little community. From words the belligerants came to blows, but they were quickly parted, and advised to settle the matter amicably, shake hands, take a quiet drink, and retire. This they did, and all who saw the fracas, supposed the affair was peacably settled.

"The next morning the Englishman took his musket or fowling-piece, loaded it with slug-shot, and stealthily repaired to the tent of the young miner, who was there, busily employed in preparing his breakfast. When he reached the entrance of the tent, the young man was standing with his back towards him, and was not aware of his approach, when the cowardly wretch raised his weapon, leveled it at the miner, and discharged its contents through his back.

"Two men who were hard by, hurried to the tent, the

murderer had no time to conceal himself. They went in and raised the dying man, heard him exclaim, 'O God! I have been murdered by that cursed English man. I saw him as I fell, with the gun in his hand.' Having articulated these words, he gasped and died.

"In an incredible short space of time, every miner within two miles of the spot, rushed to the scene of action. So quickly did they make their appearance, that one could almost imagine that they sprung up out of the earth like Satyrs.

"The murder was committed between the hours of six and seven o'clock A. M., and the miners agreed to hold a court of trial at nine o'clock the same day. The murderer was arrested, his arms pinioned, and he was securely fastened to a tree. Two miners having loaded revolvers were stationed to watch him.

"At the appointed hour the Judge with fifteen jurors, (who had been previously chosen) assembled, and the prisoner was brought before them. The charge, which was very briefly written, was read to him by the Judge, and he was asked whether he was guilty, or not guilty.

"The hardened wretch sat in dogged silence, and although his countenance indicated that he would be willing to give up a lifetime of pleasure, if he could have the opportunity to assassinate all those who were around him. Yet he opened not his mouth. Thrice was the question put to him, but he made no reply.

"The examination of the witnesses then commenced. The two witnesses who were first at the tent, after the murder had been committed, related in a lucid manner, all that then and there transpired. The Judge did not review their testimony, but put the question to a vote of hands, remarking, that every one present would be allowed to vote if they pleased. 'Now, gentlemen,' said he, 'all of you who believe that the prisoner is guilty will hold up your right hands.' Instantly, nearly all those present raised up their right hand. 'Those of a contrary mind may hold up their right hand.' Not a single hand was raised.

"The Judge then arose from his bench and addressed the prisoner. He asked him if he had anything to say before sentence was pronounced. The culprit remained in sullen silence, and would not utter a single word.

"The Judge proceeded to address the miners. He complimented them, (but I must admit that it was not in a very elegant or classical language) for their promptness of action, and the quiet manner in which they had conducted themselves during the trial, then turning to the prisoner he said:—'The sentence of the court is, that you be taken to the nearest tree, and a rope thoroughly fastened about your neck, and there hang until you are dead. And this sentence shall be executed on you within the space of forty minutes from this time!' He then added, by way of parenthesis, 'I think that will be long enough for you to settle up all your worldly affairs, and make preparations to visit another country.'

"All was now hurry and bustle among the miners, some went to procure shovels to dig a grave, others went to procure rough boards to make a box, which would be a substitute for a coffin, while another was dispatched to obtain a rope suitable to be used for the occasion.

"The prisoner with a careless, but demonical look surveyed the movements of the miners and the preparations which were being made to bring his earthly career to an abrupt close; but there were no expressions of either dread or fear pourtrayed in his countenance.

"The nearest tree stood within six or seven hundred yards of the spot where the trial was held. When the rope was brought, one of the party climbed the tree, and sitting astride a large crotchet limb he commenced removing the bark with his pocket knife, so that the rope might slide over it more easily. The limb of the tree was not more than twenty feet from the ground, but it appeared much higher. He then lowered a small cord, which was attached by those below to the end of the rope which he drew up, and then properly arranged.

"All things were now in perfect readiness, but the

forty minutes had not elapsed, fifteen minutes yet remained. The Judge who was walking about, ever and anon casting furtive glances at his watch, (which by the bye was not as large as an old fashioned warming-pan, but large enough for any able bodied man to carry about his person) appeared anxiously waiting for the minute to arrive which would free him from all responsibility and close a scene which was anything but agreeable.

While preparations were being made for the execution I approached the prisoner, and asked him if he wished to make a will, or have a letter written to any friend or relative.

"'No,' he replied, 'I don't want 'either.'

"'If,' said I, 'there is anything you wish, or any favor I can bestow, I will cheerfully grant it, if you will make it known.'

"'Then go and bring me a glass of brandy and water,' he gruffly replied.

"I complied with his request, brought the beverage, and held the tumbler to his lips while he swallowed the liquid with much apparent satisfaction.

"'Thank you,' said he, in same harsh tone of voice. 'After they have swung me up, go to my camp, and you will find there a few ounces of dust, put 'em in your pocket, and use 'em to suit yourself.'

"'That I should not be allowed to do,' was my reply,

'because all monies, or other property left by persons deceased in the mines, where they have no relatives to claim it, is used for the benefit of sick and unfortunate miners.'

"'Well,' said he, 'I don't care a d—d what's done with it, if they'd only sentenced me to be shot, and not hang'd like a Billingsgate thief, I should have felt better satisfied; but I suppose the time is almost up, and—'

"Before he had finished the sentence, two of the miners came up and conducted the culprit to the tree on which he was shortly to be suspended. The rope was adjusted around his neck. The Judge, with watch in hand, cried out, 'Gentlemen, man the rope!' Every person present, except the Judge, took hold of the rope, (some of them very reluctantly) awaiting the signal. Presently the Judge's voice was again heard in loud and distinct tones, saying, '*Gentlemen! run him up!*'

"Scarcely had the words passed from the Judges lips ere the victim was suspended high in the air. It was evident to me that the rope had not been properly fastened around his neck, and that the culprit would die by slow strangulation; the convulsive throes of the body, the swollen protruding tongue, and eyeballs starting from their sockets, together with the deathlike stillness which prevailed; all combined to make an impression on my mind which time can never efface.

"After the body had been suspended ten or fifteen minutes, it was, by order of the Judge, lowered to the ground. One of the party examined it, and said, that life was not yet extinct, as there still remained a slight pulsation of the heart.

"The Judge, who stood holding the huge watch, paused for a moment, as he gazed on the time-keeper, and remarked, '*he dies hard.*' Then raising his voice, he said: 'You must run him up again!' With an almost inconceivable rapidity, those who had hold of the rope, drew up the nearly lifeless body with such velocity that when the head struck the limb of the tree, over which the rope was drawn, the neck of the miserable victim was broken.

"Presently afterwards, the body was taken down and placed in the rough wooden box, the top of it nailed on in the same manner that a porter in a mercantile warehouse would nail up a box of goods. The box containing the body was lowered into the hole or grave, which was already prepared. The earth was quickly shoveled in, and the miners, with the Judge and jury, retired from the scene of action.

"In less than five hours after the murder was committed, the culprit had been arrested, tried, convicted, sentenced, executed and buried.

"After the execution and burial was over, each man returned to his labor. Few comments were made by any of them at the time, and in less than one week afterwards the whole affair seemed to have been entirely forgotten."

"I have," continued Uncle Zeb, "seen many executions in different parts of the world. I have seen a Spaniard sit as immovable as a statue, while the executioner was adjusting the '*Garotte.*' I have seen a Chinese who had been convicted of the crime of parricide, being prepared for the burning rack, and while the executioner was enclosing his body with the bandages which had been dipped in tar, I have listened to his piteous groans, and cries for mercy; and when the fire was lighted, have seen the poor wretch dying under the most excruciating torments;* but never yet did I witness an

---

* Years ago, the laws of China, decreed that a man who committed the crime of parricide should be burned alive. The condemned criminal was bandaged from the neck to the feet, with strips of cloth saturated with oil and tar. The body was placed in an iron frame supported by poles ten or fifteen feet long. These frames were so arranged that they could be adjusted to the body. The criminal was fastened in, with his head downwards, fire was applied to his feet, and he was left to burn out like a candle, until the body was consumed.

execution the recollection of which is so vividly impressed upon my mind as the one I have just narrated."

Let those who deprecate summary trials and executions, under what is called "Lynch Law," proclaim against them as they will. I do not intend to speak or write in vindication of them, nevertheless, there are times and circumstances which warrant the administration of prompt and speedy punishment of flagrant offenders.

The scenes enacted in one of our western cities a short time since, are fresh in the minds of the people now, and will be for many years to come. A hot blooded, pampered son of a rich man, deliberately loads his revolver, goes into a school-house, discharges the contents into the body of the teacher, and utters the most profane oaths, while his victim lies dying before him; then departs, exultingly boasting that he had shot a d—d miserable Yankee dog of a schoolmaster, who had dared to chastise his brother. The parents and relatives of the murderer were wealthy, and consequently commanded an extensive influence. The assassin was brought up for trial, the evidence against him was clear, explicit and conclusive; there was not "a loop to hang a doubt upon," nevertheless, he was acquitted. Was not this meeting out even handed justice with a vengeance?

Again, a negro on board a vessel in the harbor of New-York city, murdered the captain and crew, two or three in number, scuttled the schooner, then betook himself to a yawl-boat and went on shore. Suspicion rested upon him, he was arrested, and imprisoned to await his trial. In conversation with some of the officers and others, indubitable proofs were elicited from him, of his having committed the crime. When he was informed that persons were employed in searching for the body of the captain, he replied. "Well let them hunt, I've taken good care they shan't find him." When this man was brought up for trial, he was discharged, because the writs and legal documents contained informalities.

In the first case I have cited, it is inexplicable to me, as well as to hundreds of others, why it was that the citizens of Louisville did not seize the murderer while he was immerging from the court-house, after his acquittal, before he had an opportunity to enter the splendid carriage (that stood at the door ready to receive him,) and after giving him two new suits of clothes, one of tar, and the other of feathers, hang him up by the neck, and there let him remain long after vitality had ceased. In the other, it is possible that if the murderer, instead of a black, had worn a white skin, the informalities in the writ would have been corrected in the twinkling of an eye.

Let no one for a moment imagine that I harbor the shadow of a suspicion, that Judges or officers watch the movements of political parties, or have the slightest inclination to favor the views of those who apparently stand the best chance of being placed in a position where they can alter and revise old laws, and enact new ones, or displace Judges, and place the ermine on the shoulders of others.

In these days of peculations and defalcations, when our newspapers teem with accounts of swindling Presidents and Directors of Banks, Agents of Corporations, Bank Tellers and Clerks, are not the community at large as much in fault as the framers and administrators of the laws?

If a bank officer, or a treasurer of a corporation is detected in the commission of gross frauds, his friends will step in between him and the officers of the law, and protect him; especially when he has saved a sufficient portion of embezzled funds to make good his bondsmen, and hold them harmless. The merchant, the trader, the mechanic, and even the laborer will discuss the matter, and speak of it as an *unfortunate* affair, because he was such a nice man, and has so many respectable connections, also a young wife and interesting family, *etc.* The conclusion that the majority of the community will come to, will be, that all the circumstances considered, it would be much better to let him go than commence a prosecution. Those defaulters who commit suicide to escape the shame and ignomy of an exposure, or because they feared the prison cell, are spoken of as being very foolish weak-minded men. How often do we hear the remark made respecting such. "If he had been arrested, and tried, he never would have been convicted, unless he had squandered away all the monies he had taken."

While this state of feeling exists, justice can never overtake the wealthy murderer, incendiary, or robber; even though they are brought before our judicial tribunals.

If the rich Louisville Murderer I have alluded to, had been taken before and tried by the unlearned California Judge, and his fifteen gold-digging jurors, think you, that the plea of wealth, respectable connections, doating parents, or kind brothers and sisters, would have availed him? No, their reply would have been. He has murdered a man who never injured him. That man also had kind kindred, and fostering friends, who mourn for him, and his blood cries to us from the ground, "Justice must be done!" They would then have added. "He *shall* hang as high as Haman."

I repeat what I have already said, that I am not an advocate for "Lynch Law," but when I carefully examine such cases as I have narrated, when men who have committed the most heinous crimes are permitted to slide through the meshes of the law, on account of some informalities, or flaws in the complaints, or indictments, (nine tenths of which appear to be intentional on the part of the officers who draw them up,) and others are suffered to go at large, for no other reason except that they have rich and influential relations, and have previously borne a good character, I am inclined to think that a little of what is called "Lynch Law" would not be injurious to the interest of that portion of our citizens who support by the sweat of their brow the law-makers, and law-dispensers.

When a mechanic or laborer takes from the store or shop of his employer the most trifling article, if detected, he is brought before a magistrate, tried, convicted and punished. This is as it should be! Every honest and upright citizen will sanction it, and many aver that the court was altogether too lenient in passing sentence. The plea of respectability and former good character, will avail him nothing. The magistrate will, with much gravity inform the culprit, that in consideration of this, that, and the other, he will fix the sentence as light as the law will allow; and the prisoner is either fined, or imprisoned, getting nothing more, (perhaps less) than his just deserts.

After the employer has gone into court and testified against the employee for unlawfully appropriating to his own use and benefit, goods to the amount of twenty-five or thirty cents; he will deliberately go to those who have befriended and patronised him, and borrow money, or purchase goods to a large amount, and after having carefully laid aside a few thousand dollars, (the word *few* is so indefinite that I must leave the reader to judge what the amount would be. Some men would call three or four thousand dollars *a few*, while others would say it was a mere cypher,) he will inform his creditors that he must suspend business, and deliver up his property to them. He thinks he can pay twenty-five or thirty cents on the dollar, if he is not put to any expense; but if he is driven into chancery, the dividend would not be fifteen per cent. If his creditors agree to this, he will immediately proceed to square his accounts with them, and recommence business with his ill-gotten gains, as purse-proud as a millionaire. Is not this robbery? If I appropriate another man's property to my own use, with the preconcerted intent to defraud him, am I not as culpable as the highwayman who meets you, and orders you to stand and deliver? I am of opinion that the highwayman is the more honorable robber of the two.

I knew a young man who commenced business a few years ago, with a cash capital of four or five hundred dollars, and he was considered a shrewd, active, business man; he managed to obtain credit for more than three times that amount. By his shrewd calculations he managed to meet his notes very promptly, and for that reason he was able to get credit to a large amount. At the expiration of two years he went personally, and informed his creditors that it was necessary for him to wind up his affairs. He told them that it was with feelings of the most profound sorrow and regret, he had (after taking a careful inventory of his property,) discovered that it would not pay his creditors more than thirty cents on the dollar. Many of them believed this, and signed a document agreeing to give him a receipt in full, if the thirty per cent offered was paid within a month. The largest creditor, a shrewd old merchant, held out for a long time before he would sign this agreement, but finally said to the swindler: "I will take that, if you will pay it within an hour."

The debtor started out, saying he would borrow the amount, and very shortly returned with the money in his pocket. After paying it over and taking his receipt, he turned to the merchant and remarked: "There; now, thank God, I don't owe a man a dollar in the world, and if I had'nt dealt honest and fair I should be much better off than I am. Here I've been to work more than two years, and whether you believe it or not, I tell you, and I can prove that I've saved up only seven thousand dollars!! Hereupon he drew forth a large pocket-book, and presented before the eyes of the astonished merchant the amount named in current bank-bills.

Now, what course did this creditor pursue? Did he attempt to get the fellow indicted for swindling? No; on the contrary, he told him that he considered him a smart business man, and that his credit hereafter would be good in *his* establishment to any reasonable amount.

Cases of this kind are of a daily occurence amongst our mercantile community, but they are not so boldly executed as the one cited. Rogues and robbers are called smart. Swindlers are looked upon as shrewd business men. One half the community appear to make it their study to lay plans and adopt means to cheat the other half. "*So runs the world away.*"

WILLIAM D. EATON.

(See Page 284.)

CHAPTER XI.

How Rogues escape from Justice on account of the informalities found in indictments—A specimen of an indictment and complaint combined—Ruling of a learned Judge—The way Lawyers humbug their clients, by drawing up prolix documents—The Insanity Dodge—Physicians upon the witness stand—The way Lawyers manage to prove an Alibi—The Horse Thief who got clear, after having been convicted—A Cunning Lawyer outwitted by his more Cunning Client, &c.

I HAVE said that rogues often escape from justice and the punishment they deserve, on account of the informalities found in writs and indictments, or some legal technicalities.

Persons who have business in courts, (many, if not all of them) have noticed that whenever a prisoner is arraigned, the first thing the counsel wishes to see, is the complaint or indictment. How eagerly they will seize the document, and scan it over, trying to discover an error of omission or addition. If one is found, their eyes will glisten, and they will, in a very pompous manner, suggest to the court that their client must be set at liberty on account of the "errors in the bill." For instance:—A man is complained of for an assault and battery and is brought before a magistrate, when he is called up, the Clerk reads the complaint to him, the style and wording of which I will here note, and if I do not put it in the usual form, it will at least give the reader, (who is unacquainted with such documents,) an idea of the nonsensical prolixity of the forms of law, and of indictments.

COMMONWEALTH OF MASSACHUSETTS.

County of Suffolk, S. S

John Jones of the City of Boston, of the County aforesaid, on oath complains, that John Smith, otherwise called John Smithett, otherwise called Jonas Smithcome, otherwise called Johnny Smothface, otherwise called Jack Sneezer, did on the first day of April last past, it being in the year of our Lord 1856, with force of arms, and malice aforethought, did make an assault upon John Jones, thereby putting the said Jones in great bodily fear and terror. And the aforesaid assault made upon the said John Jones by the said John Smith, otherwise John Smithett, otherwise called Jonas Smithcome, otherwise called Jack Sneezer; he being armed with dangerous and deadly weapons. To wit:—Guns, Pistols, Swords, Daggers, Blunderbusses, Pitchforks, Shovels, Axes, Brickbats, Clubs, Stones and Staves, all against the peace and dignity of the said Commonwealth in such cases made and provided.

And the aforesaid John Jones further complains, the aforesaid assault was made upon him in the day-time.

And the aforesaid John Jones further complains, the aforesaid assault was made upon him in the night-time. And, the said Jones further declares that the aforesaid Smith held one of the aforesaid instruments in his right hand, and he further declares that the aforesaid Smith held one or more of the aforesaid instruments in both of his hands. That he did then and there beat, bruise, bang, strike, kick, and otherwise evil treat the said Jones, putting him in great bodily fear, against the peace and dignity of the Commonwealth in such case made and provided. Now, John Smith, otherwise called John Smithett, otherwise called Jonas Smithcome, otherwise called Johnny Smothface, otherwise called Jack Sneezer. What say you to this complaint? "Are you guilty, or not guilty?"*

The prisoner, after having listened attentively to the jargon of words which is read by the Court Clerk, will plead not guilty, unless he has been otherwise instructed

* The reader will perceive that I have mingled a complaint and indictment into one. They differ materially in their forms; nevertheless they are often more ridiculous than the sketch I have drawn of them.

by some two-penny lawyer, who has been engaged to defend him.

If the prisoner pleads not guilty, the witnesses are immediately called to the stand, and after having been sworn, it will be clearly shown by their testimony that the defendant John Smith, did box the ears, or slap the face of the complainant; but not until after he had been grossly abused by the complainant.

In case the defendant has no counsel, the Judge will very gravely inform him, that although he had strong provocation for committing the assault, he could not be allowed to take the law into his own hands; he should apply to the court for legal redress. If a man knocks you down in the street, you have no right to jump up, and knock him down in return. If you go home at night and find another man in bed with your wife, you have no right to chastise him, or in any way injure him; for the law will protect you, and it will also protect him.* The Judge will then inform the prisoner that there being some extenuating circumstances connected with the assault, he shall be very lenient with

---

* A learned Judge in one of the Criminal Courts of Massachusetts, while charging a jury a few months since, expressed this sentiment, in substance as I have written it: though the phrasology may be slightly altered. I marvel that his Honor did not inform the jury what course he would pursue, in case he happened to catch a poacher of this kind *sporting* in his own *preserves.*

him, an impose a fine of five dollars and costs. If the fine is not paid within two hours, the prisoner stands committed to the House of Correction.

For what purpose are indictments and other legal documents filled up, and crowded, with words and sentences, which when annalyzed signify nothing? True, these lengthy documents give employment to lawyer's and attornies' clerks, and puts money in their pockets; but they often puzzle and confound, not only the jurors, but sometimes, even the Judge himself.

We have cases upon record, where men in the ordinary walks of life, have drawn up contracts relating to important business matters, the whole condensed in simple terms, and written out in twelve or fifteen lines, on common writing paper, and I have seen documents of this discription brought into court and submitted to the Judge, who has pronounced them valid, and the juries have rendered verdicts accordingly. In any of those cases, if the contracting parties had applied to a lawyer, he would, in drawing up the document, have covered from three to seven pages of foolscap paper, closely written, and the chances are three to one, that when it was submitted to the court, it would be ruled out, and pronounced no contract at all, and the case would then be thrown out of court.

I do not pretend to say that every man is competent

to draw up a contract, or other legal document; in brief, which would stand the test of law. "The more's the pity," because those who are not capable, are the very ones who are obliged to resort to some attorney, and fee him with their hard earnings, for doing what they should be able to do themselves.

Of late years it has been a custom for lawyers whenever they take up a criminal case to defend, where the prisoner has committed some henious offence, and the evidence against the accused is so direct and clear, that there is not "a loop to hang a doubt upon," to put in the plea of insanity. This dodge is generally successful if the party is possessed of money, and has a few wealthy and influential friends; but it does not appear to work as well in the case of the poor devil who has neither. It is astonishing how quickly after a man has committed forgery, embezzled money, or taken the life of his fellow man, a number of his friends discover they have seen something wrong about him several days previous to his committing the act. One can recollect that he had seen him a few days before, stand for three consecutive minutes gazing at the weathercock on the spire of a church. Another will testify that he had seen him walking very rapidly through the streets, when he would stop suddenly, scratch his poll, then turn round and walk the other way. Another will tell you, that he has no doubt of the man's insaity, from the fact of meeting him in a drinking saloon, the week before, and there he invited two friends to imbibe at his expense; and as the man was never known to do anything of this kind before, those who witnessed the transaction were unanimous in the opinion that *something must be wrong.* Half a score of physicians, (some among them who never saw or heard of the man before,) will be called up to testify, and they will gravely inform the court, that the symptoms, as described by the witness, was satisfactory evidence, that the prisoner was laboring under some mental hallucination. The government attorney will look upon the medical gentlemen with wonder and astonishment, unable to decide in his own mind whether he is asleep or awake; he cogitates, and after his testimony is all in, he will commence his argument. But what can he say? The guilt of the prisoner is admitted; it will not do for him to animadvert, by implication or otherwise, on the testimony of the learned disciple of Galen, or Dr. Root; or attempt to impeach the well-paid witnesses for the defence. The jury will return a verdict of "not guilty, by reason of insanity," and the Judge will direct that the prisoner be removed to some lunatic asylum, there to remain until the physicians pronounce him cured.

If the culprit can dissemble, he will find it for his interest to "put an antic disposition on." This he can do very easily, and lay it aside by degrees, in a few months afterwards he will be pronounced perfectly cured, and then discharged.

Another plan which is adopted by your shrewd plotting attorney, where he finds that the "insanity dodge" will not work, is, to attempt to prove an alibi, if by any possibility the culprit can obtain a few dependable witnesses, who can be so thoroughly drilled that they will all repeat one story, and not allow themselves to be entraped by the government counsel. This drilling of witnesses is a very delicate work, and never operates well, when it is undertaken by a bungler in the profession, especially where the witnesses are not endowed with very retentive memory.

A man by the name of John Gibson Nott, a notorious horse-thief, who resided in the State of Ohio, and whose relatives were in easy circumstances, was arrested, and tried, three different times for horse-stealing, and was acquitted each time, by the shrewd management of his attorney, who in each case proved an alibi, although no one entertained a doubt with regard to the guilt of the accused.

Finally, this man stole a very beautiful and valuable horse, the property of a farmer in the vicinity. As soon as the animal was missed, suspicion rested on John Gibson Nott. The farmer employed two men to carefully watch the movements of the suspected thief, and two or three days afterwards he was seen emerging from a forest which lay a considerable distance from his dwelling. The watchers secreted themselves until he had gone out of sight, then entered the wood; after a brief search they found the horse tied to a tree, eating some provender, which appeared to have been just laid before him. The men then proceeded to inform the farmer of their discovery, who immediately sent for an officer; he, with the two assistants, secreted themselves near where the horse was tied, watching for the arrival of the thief, well knowing that he would return to feed the animal within four-and-twenty hours. They had not waited long before he made his appearance, bringing with him a pair of sheep-shears, a large knife and some cords. When he came to the spot where the horse stood, he laid down his tools, made preparations to dock the animal, and otherwise alter his appearance, by clipping him so that he might not be identified. The officer with his two assitants, who were lying in ambush close by, immediately sprang at the thief, and he was quickly arrested, and taken before a magistrate, who committed him to prison, to await his trial.

Great was the rejoicing among the people of that vicinity, when they learned that the daring and successful thief had been taken, and the evidence against him so positive, that there was no possibility of his getting clear.

Shortly after his arrest, one of the brothers went to the attorney who had defended him on the former occasions, and requested him to take hold of this case.

"No!" was the reply, "I got the rascal acquitted three times, and in this case there is no defence. I'll have nothing more to do with him."

The brother urged the attorney strongly; but he was inexorible.

"I'll give you three hundred dollars!"

"No, you'd better keep your money, I can't help him."

"I'll give you four hundred dollars!"

"No!"

"I'll give you five hundred dollars!"

The attorney hesitated a few moments, and then replied.

"Well, pass over your money, and I'll see what I can do!"

The money was paid, and the man left the attorney's office.

When it became known that this cunning counsellor had agreed to defend the villain for the fourth time, and as he had been heard to say repeatedly that he would never again appear in court to defend the rascal, under any circumstances, some of the people came to the conclusion that he must be insane.

The day of trial came. The court-house was filled. The counsel for the prisoner appeared to take less interest in the proceedings than the spectators in the courtroom. His cross-examination of the government witnesses was very concise. In his plea to the jury, he briefly asserted, that there was no testimony adduced which could criminate the prisoner, and he was satisfied he would be honorably acquitted.

Before the trial was concluded, the counsellor for the prisoner took the brother aside, and told him to obtain a fleet horse, saddled and bridled, bring him there, and stand by his side near the court-house door. The jury retired, but were not long in finding a verdict. When they returned to their seats, the Judge asked if they had agreed upon a verdict. The foreman answered in the affirmative. The prisoner was ordered to stand up and look upon the foreman as he rendered the decision. The foreman in a clear and distinct voice, said: "The verdict of this jury is, John Gibson Nott; *Guilty*.

"Just as I expected," shouted the attorney for the prisoner, "John Gibson, NOT GUILTY."

Mr. John Gibson Nott, took his que from the lawyer, and then took to his heels. He bounded out of the court-house, leaped upon the back of the horse which stood in waiting for him at the door, and before the astonished court and officers recovered their equilibrium, the lucky prisoner was out of sight.

John was never again seen in that vicinity.

The Judge ordered the counsellor to be arrested, but when he was brought to trial, there was no law to be found that would reach his case, he had only repeated the words of the foreman of the jury.

Occasionally some of these shrewd lawyers are themselves out-witted by their clients.

A man who had stolen a horse and chaise, and sold the same, was arrested and brought to trial. He stipulated with a cunning lawyer to defend him, agreeing to pay him fifty dollars if he was acquitted.

The lawyer instructed his client how to act, and what to say, when he was brought into court. The fellow profited by his advice. When he was arraigned, and placed upon the stand to hear the indictment read, he took from his pocket a child's picture book, and with an idiotic look appeared much interested gazing at the prints. When he was asked whether he plead guilty, or not guilty, he burst out with a loud laugh, saying, "See that little d—d hedge-hog under the fence," then holding up the book, and looking at the Judge, he exclaimed, "O! look here! just tell your mother to come here a minute."

The Judge turned to the Clerk, and asked "Is not that man *non compos mentis*."

The lawyer arose and assured his Honor, that such was the fact. That the poor fellow had strayed from home, (stating the place where he belonged) and that one of his relatives who was searching for him had just arrived, and was there in the court, and he wished to have him put upon the witness stand to testify and coroborate the fact.

The witness, (who was an accomplice of the thief,) swore that he had known the poor unfortunate creature from his childhood, that he was perfectly harmless, and when at home was carefully watched, to prevent him straying away.

The Judge ordered him to be discharged.

The lawyer was elated at the success of his plan. He followed the prisoner and his accomplice out of the court-house, and when they reached a spot where they could not be overheard he congratulated his client, and requested him to "fork over" the amount promised him for his services.

The thief resumed his idiotic look, and produced the picture-book which the lawyer had given him, and held it up before the attorney, exclaiming, "Don't you see that little d—d hedge-hog under the fence?"'

"Capital trick warn't it, and shrewdly managed?" exclaimed the attorney.

"Just tell your mother to come here a minute," was the response.

"You played your part remarkable well," said the lawyer.

"Did *you* see that little d—d hedge-hog under the fence?" rejoined the client.

"Let us throw off this foolery now," said the lawyer, "because I am in haste. Pay me what you agreed to, and I shall be glad to defend you again."

The client placed his mouth close to the ear of the attorney, and shouted loud enough to wake old "Enceladus," *O look here! Tell your mother to come here a minute.*"

The attorney turned upon his heel and started. Whether he ever tried "the picture-book game" again, deponent saith not.

CHAPTER XII.

Character of Court Witnesses as delineated when they are upon the witness stand—The Reckless Witness—The Temperance Man who was a hard drinker—Infidel Witness—The Infidel who refused to take an oath—The way that Judges and Jurors are often deceived—The Superstitious Witness—The Interpreter Witness—Novel defence of an Irish Witness—The Comical Negro Witness—Penalties for Perjury—Loafers and Procurers for Brothels who are hangers on in the Court Rooms, &c.

THOSE who would study the different phases of the human character, as indicated by the looks, words, and actions of men, cannot have a better school than the court-rooms. If a person visits them and carefully watches the witnesses as they are brought upon the stand to testify, they will learn more of human nature in one day, than they could in months elsewhere. It is my belief that there is not one witness out of twenty, either in the civil or criminal courts, who when they are brought up to render in their evidence are entirely disinterested, unbiased, and unprejudiced. I do not mean to say that the majority of witnesses are dishonest, and deliberately misrepresent facts and matters connected with the case, or cases on trial, but I do say that it is almost impossible for any one to render in a fair, correct and impartial evidence, when they are in any way prejudiced either for, or against a man, or any body of men, who may have a trial pending.

This prejudice extends not only to individuals, but often witnesses will harbor strong prejudices either for, or against a particular nation, and its inhabitants generally. If a foreigner, especially if he was so unfortunate as to first look upon the light in the green "Isle of Erin," has been charged with committing any offence, and the witnesses called to testify against him are Americans, who believe that there are more foreigners in the country than there should be, think you that their evidence in the case would be the same that it would if a friend or acquaintance of their's instead of the Irishman had committed the same offence, and was placed in precisely the same situation? Reverse the case and you will have the same results.

When a police officer arrests a man for some violation of law, and goes into court to testify against him, it is not for his interest to have the man acquitted. If he is, it implies a false arrest, tending to show by implication that the officer does not know his duty, and is not a fit man for the situation; consequently he is led to swear (as the Butcher Boys say,) "way up to the handle."

Then we have the careless, reckless witness, who will for fifty cents go upon the stand and swear to almost any thing, and every thing, that may be required of him, without having the least compunctions of conscience; on the contrary, he will go among his companions afterwards and boast of having "pulled the wool over the eyes" of the Judge, and that he did'nt know much about the case, but what he did'nt know, he guessed at. Such witnesses are near akin to the deliberate systematic perjurer, who goes into court with the full determination to pile lie upon lie, until his falsehoods become countless, if by so doing he can further his own interests or those of his friends.

A man who resided in the eastern part of Massachusetts, was a few years ago summoned to appear in court, in a case where a friend of his was on trial for selling spirituous and intoxicating liquors. When this man was called upon the witness stand, in answer to the first question asked by the government counsel, which was:

"Do you know the defendant?"

He deliberately answered,

"No, I never saw him but twice in my life."

When asked if he ever visited the defendants place of business, he replied,

"I have been there once or twice."

But when the question was put to him whether or not

he ever drank any intoxicating liquors in the defendants premises, he boldly declared that he never had any, furthermore, had no recollection of ever drinking a drop of spirituous or intoxicating liquors in his life, before that day.

The government counsel well knowing that the witness had been in the habitual use of liquors for many years, appeared much surprised at this answer.

"Then you acknowledge you have drank spirituous liquors to-day," remarked the counsellor.

"Yes," was the reply, "I thought I'd try a little today just to see how it seemed."

"How many times have you drank to day?" was the next question asked him. The witness stood for some moments apparently calculating the number of libations, and finally answered,

"I can't recollect exactly but I think I have drank about *twenty-five or thirty times*!"*

"That's beginning pretty strong for a Temperance man, I should think," replied the counsellor. "Where did you obtain this large number of drinks?"

---

*Incredible as it may appear, there were many persons in the Court House at the time, who knew the man, and believed that this statement was correct, although there was no symptoms of inebriation which showed themselves either in the looks, words, or actions of the witness. It was about four o'clock in the afternoon when he was called to the stand.

"Oh! I got them in different places," was the answer. "You don't suppose a man would drink as many times as that in one place, do you?"

"Mention the name of one place where you drank?" said the counsellor.

"Couldn't do it," was the reply. "I ain't much acquainted round town, but I've got an awful slew of friends about here, and every one of them I met, would say to me, 'Come let's go and take something to take.' Then, I'de tell them, guess not; 'cause I'de joined a Temperance Society. Then I'de think better on't, and go in and smile two or three times, just to please them. I'm one of the most accommodating men you ever did see."

"You can't recollect a single place where you drank. Now sir, can you remember where you eat your dinner to-day?"

"Yes sir, it was up to the —— Hotel. I sat at the table near you, and said to a friend of mine; says I, that's the County Attorney, and I pointed you out to him, because I knewed that you'd be inquiring into all my family affairs, and I made out a list of all the relations I could think of, so as not to put you to much trouble. You said to a gentleman who sat opposite to you, that you expected to hear some terrible hard swearing this afternoon, and I mistrusted you were more than half right, because the world is so awfully given to lying!"

"Did you drink any liquor at the hotel where you ate dinner?" asked the counsellor.

"No!" replied the witness, "I happened to find out that they charged a shilling a drink there, and I couldn't stand that, any how."

"You say that you never drank a drop of intoxicating liquor in your life before to day, and that you belong to a Temperance Society. Now, when did you join, and why did you join, that society?"

"I can't tell exactly when; but the reason why, was to please old Parson B—— and my wife. They said if I'de only jine that institution it would have a great influence on the young and rising generation. So you see, to please them I jined."

"Well sir," said the counsellor, "you can sit down."

The witness left the court-room in company with a friend, with the avowed intention of trying to ferret out one of those places where intoxicating liquors were sold, and obtaining the proprietors card, that he might hereafter produce it, in case he should ever again be called to the witness stand.

There is another class of witnesses who often cause considerable trouble in our courts of law. I allude to those who have expressed and promulgated what are called, Infidel's sentiments and doctrines. In many of the States this class of people are not allowed to testify in the courts, or in other words their evidence is not admitted.

I have often seen a Judge very much perplexed, and undecided in his own mind, whether or not to allow the testimony of one who called himself a free-thinker, when the opposing party have objected to its admission. I do not intend to express any opinion respecting this or any other law which interferes with a man's religious opinions. I have seen men who were professed Infidels whose testimony I would readily take, and believe; and I regret to say that I have seen others who were *professed* Christians, whose testimony I would reject and disbelieve, even if they were standing upon a thousand bibles, with their right hand held up towards heaven. It appears to me that a man's moral character, his good, or evil habits, and the estimation in which he is held by his fellow men, should be the criterion by which to estimate and judge of the truth or falsity of his testimony, not his Theological views and opinions.

I have in my mind a case in point. A young man about twenty two or three years of age was summoned to appear in court to testify in a very important case, which was then pending. The plaintiff knowing how he would testify, and fearing that if his testimony was admitted he would lose his case, objected to his going upon the witness stand, on the ground that he was an Infidel, and consequently his testimony was inadmisable.

The Judge called the young man to him, and asked, "are you an Infidel?"

The reply was. "Your Honor in the common acceptation of the word Infidel *I am*; but if you will allow me, I will give you very briefly my views on the subject of Theology, and then you will be able to decide whether or not my evidence can be admitted."

The young man was of preposessing appearance, and would be taken by some for a juvenile Methodist Preacher. He commenced in an off-hand way to deliver a regular Theodore Parker sermon. He had not proceeded far before the Judge checked him, and ordered the Court Clerk to administer the oath to him.

The Clerk told him to hold up his right hand, this he peremptorily refused to do.

The Judge asked him why he refused to take the oath.

"I have conscientious scruples," was the reply.

"Will you affirm?" continued the Judge.

"Most certainly your Honor," was the answer.

After having gone through the form of affirmation, he gave in his testimony with such conciseness, and apparent honesty, that the Judge appeared to look and act as though he would like to have "Infidel witnesses of *his* stamp" whenever important cases were brought before him for adjudication.

There are another class of men who when they appear in court, and are called up to testify, may with propriety be termed, imprudent witnesses. Such persons are for the most part well meaning, and honest, so far as their prejudices will allow them to be, but they will generally get excited and irritable, especially when cross-examined by some aggravating lawyer, who uses every means in his power to annoy and make them contradict themselves. In the Civil Courts many a man who has had a case in litigation, when it would have resulted otherwise, if some one, or more of his witnesses had been more calm and judicious. When a witness loses his temper, the party who has brought him upon the witness stand will oftentimes lose their case, which might have resulted very differently if the witness in giving their testimony had used more discretion.

It is very annoying I grant for a man to be called into court against his will, and be kept upon a witness stand an hour or more, while some scrub lawyer is cross-questioning him, and attempting to brow beat and intimidate him.

In reading an account of a trial in one of our courts, where one of these sixpenny lawyers was engaged. I was much amused at the answers given by a gentleman in reply to questions put to him by the attorney. During the cross-examination the witness was calm, cool, and collected, although the attorney resorted to all possible means to make him contradict himself; but after he found that all his efforts were futile, he laid back in his chair, and looking the witness directly in the face, he said: Now sir, I want to ask you if you was ever in the State's Prison?"

"Yes sir, I have been there," was the prompt reply.

"The Court and Jury will please take note of that," the lawyer exultingly responded.

"And when did you come out of the State Prison?" was the next question.

"It was about four months ago," was the reply. I think it was on the fifteenth of June last. I recollect going in with some of my friends and seeing you there. I asked the warden why you was not dressed in uniform like the rest of the prisoners. You see, I made a slight mistake; *I took you for one of the convicts.*"

This witness might with propriety be classed among the self-possessed and safe witnesses. But with these even, both the Judge and jury are often led astray.

At the trial of a case in the Supreme Court of Massachusetts, Chief Justice Shaw presiding, where a large amount of property was involved, the most important witness for the plaintiff was summoned by the defendant, and the case rested entirely upon his testimony. Great was the astonishment of the counsel for the defence, when this man was brought upon the witness stand to hear him give in his evidence cooly and concisely in favor of the plaintiff. The Judge in reviewing the case dwelt very strongly upon the testimony of this witness, remarking that it was rendered with so much care and precision, that there could not be a doubt in the mind of any who heard it, respecting its fairness and impartiality. In fact the Judge complimented the witness, which was something unusual for him under any circumstances. But afterwards the fact became known to a few, that if the plaintiff gained his case, this *honest* witness would be benefited to the amount of two or three hundred dollars.

Thus we see that the Judge and jurors are often deceived by those who appear to be the most honest and impartial witnesses.

We will now glance at the superstitious witness. One of this class will often go into court with great dread and fear of testifying to more, or less than the truth, and sometimes their testimony amounts to just nothing at all. In testifying they will add to their answers, and to every question asked, clauses like this. "Well I think so, but I ain't certain." "I believe so and so, was so and so; but I can't swear positively," &c. Witnesses of this kind may as well be kept out of court as to be brought in, for their evidence amounts to nothing, unless corroborated by other testimony.

Some females who are firm adherents to the Roman Catholic Church, believe that they would be committing a great sin by taking an oath while they were *enciente.*

Females of this class will resort to almost any expedient to avoid a witness' summons, or be brought into a court-room. I have seen some of this class, who when called upon to testify refuse to take the oath, and fall down upon their knees, begging the Judge to excuse them, and with twenty oaths, protesting that they will tell the whole truth, if the Judge will only listen to them, and not oblige them to swear on the Holy Evangelist. But after the Judge has sentenced one of them to fifteen days imprisonment in the common jail, for non-compliance with the rules of the court, they will suddenly alter their minds, and express their willingness to swear to any thing, and every thing that may be required, rather than to take a journey to the prison cell in the "Black Maria." But they generally speak too late; the fiat has gone forth, and is irrevocable; for the Judge will say, that the very fact of the woman's refusal in the first place to take the required oath, and afterwards finding that she must be incarcerated, clearly showed that it was not from conscientious scruples that she refused, and therefore the penalty should be awarded. Such decisions are hard I grant, but somebody must be taken, and held up as examples, to intimidate the reckless ones, who when they are brought into court, either perjure themselves while testifying, or those superstitious people who refuse to testify under oath.

No man can go into court when he is arraigned for violation of any law, by pleading ignorance, and escape the penalties of such violations, whatever it may be. If a man is arraigned for drunkenness, or any other petty offence, the plea of non-knowledge of the laws, cannot, and will not save him, although it may be taken in extenuation, by both Judge and jury in the higher courts, and by the Justice or Recorder of the lower courts. He cannot escape the penalties of the law, in such cases made and provided.

It is no pleasant task for me after having watched very carefully for more than five years, the courts and all that are connected therewith, to chronicle the known fact, that our Courts of Justice, or in other words that *should* be Courts of Justice, are oftentimes made a stage, upon which trickery, and villainy hang around the curtains of the benches; and witnesses are there ready to swear to any thing; with accomplices standing without the porch, watching for an opportunity to swindle a stranger, or dishonestly obtain a dollar.

There is another style of witness who are often called into court, who instead of being ridiculed, and laughed at, as they usually are, should be treated with kind consideration and respect. I allude to those witnesses who do not understand the English language. They know nothing of our laws, manners, or customs, and are obliged to give in their testimony with an interpretor at their side, who nine times out of ten misinterprets their language. Every judicious magistrate will take the testimony of such witnesses with much caution, and will scarcely receive it at all, unless corroborated by other evidence.

The most mirth provoking class of witnesses that are brought into our courts, are the genuine newly imported Hibernians. As a general thing when they will testify at all, (sometimes it is almost impossible to get a word out of them,) they will repeat their story so rapidly and introduce so many cant phrases, (the meaning of which is known only to themselves,) that it is almost impossible for the Judge, counsel, or jurymen, to elicit the truth, however well disposed, or honest the witness may be.

An Irishman who had been arrested for stealing a piece of meat from a butcher's stall, was brought to trial, and one of his countrymen appeared as a witness for the defence. When he was brought up to the witness stand, he was asked if he knew the prisoner.

"Be Jabers, you may well be saying that same. I knew him in the ould country, or ever I came to Amereky, and a broth of a boy he was sure, divil a bit of a row was he ever in, only when he'd take a wee drop of whiskey too much, and a wild fellow he was among the girls too when he—"

"Stop! stop!" exclaimed the counsellor," what do you know about this larceny?"

"And what the divil do you call that?" returned Pat, scratching his head and looking bewildered.

"What do you know about the stealing of the meat from the butcher's stall, which this man is charged with?"

"Och! its the stealing of the mate that your after being finding out about, is it?" replied Pat. "I know all about it, and sure. The boy has only been in this country two wakes Good Friday, and didn't myself entirely take him from the ship on the wharf, and wasn't I after keeping him in my own cellar every blessed hour since. And be Jabers, divil a bit of mate have we had to ate, at all at all, only some herring and baked paraties is all the mate we had to put into our mouths this many a day, and I can prove it, for der you see, I have 'em all here in me pocket."

Hereupon Pat thrust his hands into his capacious coat-pockets, and drew forth a few red herrings and a half dozen cold baked potatoes, which he held up triumphantly before the court, imagining that that was a clincher, and that his friend would be immediately discharged. Great was the astonishment of Pat when he heard his comrade sentenced to the House of Correction, notwithstanding he had testified mighty strong in his favor.

When a genuine African, or one of African descent, who knows nothing of our courts of law, is brought upon the witness stand to testify, he will, (or some of them will) annoy the court and amuse the spectators, especially one who had just emigrated from the cotton-fields of the South.

This class of witnesses are very polite and obsequious, not knowing what titles to apply to the different court officers, they will call a policeman "Your Honor," and the judge "General." In most cases, the testimony of this class of witnesses is to be relied on, because they suppose that a fearful penalty will be imposed upon them if they deviate from the truth.

During the examination of one of these "sable sons," an attorney, during his cross-examination, asked the witness where he belonged.

"I come from old Virginia, your honor," was the answer.

"Well, and whose slave are you?" asked the counsellor.

"When I was dar I was Colonel Strickland's slave; but, bress the Lor', I'se my own niggah now. Yah! yah!" The free darkey shook his sides with laughter, as he took a mental retrospective view of his previous condition as compared with the situation in which he was now placed; many of the court officers and spectators involuntary joined the colored witness in his cachinations.

It is a well-known fact, that there are many persons brought into court, to testify in cases of great importance, as well as those of a lesser grade, who do not understand the nature of an oath. Examples of this kind are not uncommon even in the courts of New England; and, I believe, the time is not far distant, when the administration of oaths in all our courts will be entirely abolished, and, instead thereof, the affirmation substituted. As the laws and customs now are, we have one form of oath for the Protestant, another for the Catholic, and another still for the Quaker, and so on.

Now, I have had some experience in the courts, and have carefully watched all grades and classes of witnesses, as they have, from time to time, rendered their testimony, and never yet, in a single instance, seen a witness upon the stand who, to the best of my belief, gave in his, or her testimony, with any more truth and honesty than they would have done, had not the oath been administered unto them.

If the laws regulating the administration of oaths were abolished, and the form of affirmation substituted in their stead, I would have the pains and penalties which now follow the conviction of the crime of perjury more stringent than they now are, and such penalties should be more rigidly enforced than they are at the present time.

In the year 1855, Justice Russell, of the Police Court of Boston, bound over seven or eight persons who had perjured themselves upon the witness stand of the lower court, and held them under bonds of two or three hundred dollars for their appearance in the upper court. If I have been correctly informed, not one of the whole number was arraigned for the very good reason that the Grand Jury found no bill against them.

What a farce is this? A law which was enacted for the greater protection of the lives, liberties, and property of the community, stands a dead letter upon the Statute Book, and we seldom hear of a man's being tried and convicted of the crime of perjury, no matter how palpable the proofs may be against him.

Speaking of the indefinite knowledge that many persons have respecting the nature of an oath, recalls to my mind an incident which occurred in the city of London some three or four years ago, where an old man who was between sixty and seventy years of age was brought before a magistrate, to testify in some petty case. Some one informed his Honor, that the witness did not understand the nature of an oath; and the magistrate, after having asked a few questions, was perfectly satisfied that he did not. Finally, the magistrate asked him if he knew there was a God, who directed and governed all things.

"Yes," replied the witness; "I'se hearn of him often enough; but, you see, I'se to work down in the coal-pits all the time; went down when I was a boy, and a'int been to Lun'un but once afore for thirty years. So you see every time the old chap comes round here, I don't get no chance go get a squint at him. They said he was down round Liverpool a spell ago; but I didn't see him."

If this was not an incontrovertible fact, I would not chronicle it. It only goes to show that the old maxim, "One half the world don't know how the other half live," is correct, and that there is more truth than poetry in the words.

A little boy between seven and eight years of age was brought into one of our courts, to testify in a case of considerable importance, which was then and there pending. The counsel for one of the parties objected to the boy's testimony being received on account of his extreme youth, and the impossibility of his comprehending the nature of an oath. The magistrate asked the child, who was a very intelligent looking and active lad, if he knew what an oath was.

"Yes, sir," replied the boy.

And do you know what punishment will be awarded, if you do not tell the truth?" continued the magistrate.

"Yes sir." Joe Gibbs told me, that if I didn't tell the truth when you got me up here, I'd go to hell d—d quick."

The testimony of the lad was admitted.

From what I have already said, the reader will perceive that there is but little reliance to be placed on the testimony of a major part of the witnesses who are brought upon the stand where their evidence (if taken) will either acquit, or convict, the accused parties who are brought before our criminal courts, or turn the scale in cases of civil action.

Both judges and jurors are sworn to render verdicts according to law and evidence; and those who most religiously adhere to their oaths and dispense justice accordingly are often so deceived that they unwittingly allow the guilty to escape, and sometimes punish the innocent for the offences committed by others who possess more cunning and knowledge than themselves.

There are thousands of females in the community who would and do, suffer wrongs and insults rather than go into court, and make a complaint, or be called on to the witness stand to testify, where they are sure to find some lecherous, pettifogging lawyer standing ready to browbeat, and put improper and indecent questions to them before a large crowd of people, most of whom are loafers of the lowest class, having no lawful calling or reputable business.

A large proportion of these pests are procurers for brothels, and are supported by, and with the wages of sin and iniquity. If a young girl is brought up for some petty larceny and has no friends to plead in her behalf, they will offer to pay the fine imposed and furnish her with a good home and comfortable lodgings. The girl must decide between the prison and the brothel, and will generally accept the latter. With the vile associates that she must necessarily come in contact with, together with the infamy attached to her name, her downward course is very rapid. No friend to advise, no opportunity to leave a den of infamy, and again establish a character and a respectable position in society, she drags out the few brief years of a miserable existence, and is then consigned to the "Potter's field."

No feasable plan has yet been devised to check and

punish these brothel procurers; but here comes my uncle Zeb, and I will consult him on the subject.

Listen, while I repeat his advice.

"My dear boy," said he, "the best way is to let this class of people alone, because they are so closely connected with men of capital who own large amounts of real estate, and, who, by the means of these people, receive fifteen or twenty per cent. interest on their real estate, which is a portion of their ill-gotten gains, whereas, without them, they would only receive six or seven per cent.; and, whereas, these landlords have great power and influence, which their wealth brings to them, it is the height of folly to wage war against those who fill their capacious coffers. I tell thee, boy, that it is folly to war against crime, where you are obliged to contend with men of wealth and influence."

Musing for a few moments, I concluded that the old gentleman was right, and as the great poet has said,

> "Let Hercules himself do what he may,
> The cat will mew, the dog will have his day,"

I concluded to turn to another subject.

CHAPTER XIII.

The Laws of Divorce—The Author's idea with regard to the rites of marriage—The law protecting dumb beasts more stringent than those enacted to protect females who happen to be ill-mated—The deleterious effects which ill-timed marriages have upon the community—Decisions of the Supreme Court of the United States respecting marriage-contracts—The laws pertaining to rape—The opinion and decision of Queen Elizabeth in a case brought before her—Seductions—The advantages the woman has over the man, in all such cases, as the laws are framed, &c.

ALTHOUGH the laws pertaining to marriage are very nearly alike in every State in the Union, the laws pertaining to divorce, in the several States, differ very materially.

A priest, Minister of the Gospel, (as it is dispensed by the Protestants;) and your addle-headed and half-witted Justices of the Peace, have authority to perform the marriage ceremony, and declare two persons of different sexes man and wife. Many of them will, with all gravity, wind up the performance by saying: "What God has joined together, let no man put asunder." But all the Priests, Ministers and Justices in Christendom cannot unloose the knot which the meanest of them can tie.

The laws respecting divorce, although they differ in almost every State, are so absurd and ridiculous that the sooner they are altered and amended, the better it will be for the community.

Ill-timed and ill-advised marriages are and ever have been a prolific source of trouble and misery to all who are unequally yoked together, and it will be always so, until the laws of divorce are materially altered. These laws have affected people of all grades and classes, from the king upon the throne, down through the whole ramifications of society, to the poorest cottager. The priest and minister will tell you that the marriage rites and laws are a Heaven-ordained institution, while the Supreme Court of the United States tells you, that the marriage vows amount to nothing more, nor less, than a civil contract; and that august body has decided that if a man takes to himself a woman, by her own free will and consent, and the man acknowledges, before two or more witnesses, that the woman *is* his wife, and not his concubine, the marriage is valid, and the woman is entitled to all the rights and privileges of a wife, also, to the lawful proportion of whatever property the man may possess at the time of his demise, should she outlive him, and her offspring, if any there be, from such union, are legitimate children, and legal heirs.

Now if the decision of these Solon umpires is correct, and will stand the test, is marriage, of itself, anything more or less than a civil contract, which binds the parties who have thus entered into a co-partnership? If the words in that contract should read: "so long as you both can *agree*," instead of "so long as you both do *live*," I am of opinion that much of the misery which is entailed upon the children by the fathers and mothers, unto the third and fourth generation, would be mitigated, if not abated.

I know that many will say that if sentiments like these were promulgated throughout the community, they would strike a death-blow to all our civil institutions, and every town and city would shortly become corrupted, and become a nest of foul and unclean birds. It is very easy to make assertions, but not so easy to prove them. Let us look at the law as it is; a man cannot get a divorce from his wife, unless one or the other of the parties are able to prove desertion, adultery, or the commission of some criminal offence, which must be brought before the Judges of the Supreme Court, and there publicly investigated, with a score of reporters, who sit ready to note down every circumstance, the testimony of every witness, the questions put by impertinent lawyers, the looks, appearance and contour of both parties, necessarily obliged as they are, to dress up everything in the most fantastic robes, as they cater for the depraved taste of the community.

A vast amount of paper, and an incredible quantity of printer's ink will be used to inform the world that Mrs. Jones, suspecting that her leige lord and husband, Mr. Jones, had been, and was too familiar with Mrs. Smith, and as she had watched his movements, and found that Jones visited Smith at sundry times, and in divers manners, and on one occasion the said Jones was found in close proximity with the said Smith, she applies for a divorce from his bed and board.

All matters of this kind are readily caught up and discussed by a large portion of the community. The minister of the gospel leaves his half-written sermon to ponder over the libidinous report; the staid merchant, in his counting-room, will carefully examine it, before he reads the report of prices of stock on 'Change; the antiquated damsel of fifty years, who always hated the men, because they were such treacherous and deceitful creatures; and the fastidious Miss, who has carefully perused the paper, while closeted in her chamber, will take it to her maternal parent, exclaiming:

"O! Ma; just read and see what naughty folks the 'Smith's' and 'Jones' are." Then add:

"The paper says they've been doing something which they hadn't 'orter, and I want you to tell me all about it."

Shakespeare, who is supposed to have known something of human nature, said:

"I'd rather be a toad, and feed upon the vapor of a dungeon,
Than keep a corner in the thing I love, for others' uses."

How many thousands and tens of thousands there are, who have come upon the stage, and fretted away a few brief hours, since the "Bard of Avon" chronicled this sentence, who have uttered and reiterated these words, and unborn millions will repeat the sentiment, until that epoch shall arrive, (which has been spoken of by the Rev. John Todd, and other equally distinguished men,) when the mighty angel shall descend from heaven, and place one foot upon the dry land, and the other upon the sea, and swear by Him who sitteth upon the throne, that time shall be no longer. Where those Rev. gentlemen obtained their information respecting this novel and curious procedure, which they aver will shortly come to pass, is entirely beyond my comprehension. I should not be willing to believe it without a consideration, cash in hand, paid.

To return to the subject of divorces, I will remark, that, in my humble belief, Heaven never ordained any institution, nor any laws, which would oblige two persons to live together, whose dispositions, tastes, manners and habits are diametrically at variance, and who cannot and will not enjoy each other's society. What would be said of a State Legislature who enacted a law which allowed men to put animals together in one and the same cage, whose natural antipathy to each other was such that they would, under any and every circumstance, fight until one or the other of them were destroyed? The world would protest against such infamous barbarity, as being revolting to the better nature of man. But when these Legislators enact laws which bind together two human beings, and oblige them to live together in the same house, cage, or dwelling, during the term of their natural lives, that is pronounced right and proper, because, forsooth, by so doing they are regulating this Heaven-ordained institution.

I anticipate and hear the reader say that men and women are not animal brutes, but beings, endowed with faculties, intellects, and immortal souls. This I grant, and here I will take you on the argument.

Men are intellectual beings, but that intellectuality which they possess, (or, I should say, which some of them possess,) governing as it does the material body, and the animal passions therewith connected, will often throw aside everything which we call reason and propriety. If at one time love and affection are the dominant passions, it does not follow that hatred, and disgust, may not fill their places. You may have a great regard and affection for a man to day, and be willing to entrust him with untold gold, but to-morrow you may discover that he is an arrant knave and swindler, whose society you would shun. You may see to-day a female that you believe to be an angel, and imagine that if you can prevail upon her to be your companion through life, and smooth its rough edges, as you "toddle down the vale of time," you will be the happiest man in existence; to-morrow you find that you are indissolubly bound to a female devil incarnate, who will make your home a hades and your life miserable. Nevertheless, she is your wife and you have entered into a co-partnership which death alone can dissolve, unless you go deliberately forth, and commit some crime which will consign you to the State's Prison.

On the other hand, a trustful and confiding maiden becomes enamored of a man whom she knows little or nothing about. He proposes to marry her, and is accepted. Shortly afterwards, she discovers that he is a worthless scamp, who would, for a few dollars, make a prostitute of her, and by so doing he can obtain funds to squander in brothels or at the gaming-table. She must submit, and drink the cup of misery to its dregs, while her relatives, and those who had before professed to be her friends, will pass her by with a jest and a jeer, saying: "As she has made her bed, so let her lie on it."

We have examples of this kind before our eyes every day. We see persons whose temperaments and dispositions are as different as daylight from darkness, who are bound together by a tie that nothing but death, the Supreme Court, or the Legislature, can unloose.

But it is not alone upon these ill-mated couples that the misfortune comes. After the halcyon days which follow 'love's' (I beg pardon, I should have said 'passion's') young dream are over, scions will often arise, upon whose future growth and trainng much depends. They may be reared and instructed so that they will become ornaments and blessings to the world, or objects of pity, shame and disgrace. What can be expected of a family of children who see nothing from day to day but bickerings, turmoils and quarrels, between their progenitors? Do not many of them, as they come to mature years, like the patriarch Job, curse the day and hour that gave them birth, and often flee from the unhappy roofs and fire-sides of their parents, for no other reason than to escape from scenes of strife which they do not wish to witness? Most certainly there is. Thousands of such cases are occurring daily among us, the major part of which are unknown to the community at large; nevertheless, their pernicious tendencies are felt, both directly and indirectly, and influence all grades of society.

If a man beats, bruises, and ill-treats a horse, he is arrested, examined, and sent up for trial to a higher court, where he will be tried by a jury, and if convicted, the Judge will sentence him to pay a fine of fifty or one hundred dollars, or three or four months imprisonment in the Penitentiary. But if he abuses, beats, and evil treats his wife, he is taken before a magistrate, and if it appears in evidence that he has not maimed her, by breaking a limb, ruined her eyesight for life, nor used any dangerous and deadly weapon in his assault, he is fined three dollars and costs of court, and perhaps put under fifty dollars bonds to keep the peace for three months.

Thus, according to the laws as they now stand, a man can abuse and beat his wife, and if he is called up to answer for the offence, (which not one out of a hundred are,) he is sure of getting off by the payment of a small fine, even though the woman by marrying him may have raised a mortal (not to the skies, but from the gutter,) while he, instead of elevating, has dragged an angel down; but if this brute in human form undertakes to chastise a vicious horse, the prison-gates are opened to receive him, if he should be complained of and brought to trial.

An English nobleman, who visited this country a few years ago, was asked by one of his friends what his impressions were respecting the same. After a few moments of deliberation, he replied:

"From what slight observations I have had an opportunity to take, I am inclined to believe that it is a heaven for women, but a hell for horses."

If this foreigner had visited our Police and Recorder's Courts a few times, he would probably have altered his opinion, and materially changed his views.

In all cases where an application is made for a divorce,

the female, though she be as cursed as "Socrates' Xantippe," will, if she has a winning way, and pleasing smile, gain the sympathy not only of the Judge on the Bench, but also of the whole community. The case of a celebrated tragedian of this country, who a short time since attempted to get a divorce from his wife, on the ground of adultery, fully demonstrates this. I know not, neither do I care whether the woman was innocent or guilty, but I do know that nine-tenths of the community (or, I should say, the male portion of the community,) appeared disposed to pronounce the woman guiltless, and contend that they believe that she was more sinned against than sinning. With the female portion it is different; they will as strongly assert that they consider the man free from all blame, and that if he had been guilty of any indiscretions, he had been driven to them by the woman, after he found that she was false.

If the laws of divorce had been so framed that one or both of these well known individuals could have gone before a Supreme Justice, and the Justice had been endowed with power to grant a dissolution of the unhappy co-partnership, without obliging the man to criminate the woman, and the woman to re-criminate in turn, would not both the man and woman have both been far better and happier than they now are? If such was the case, all that the community would have known (and which was no benefit whatever for them to know respecting the domestic affairs of others,) would have amounted to this, and this only:

" The co-partnership heretofore existing between Mr. Edwin ———, and Mrs. Catherine ———, is hereby dissolved, by mutual consent."

The only punishment that should be inflicted upon a man who unwittingly runs his neck into the matrimonial noose, should be to oblige him to support the woman, (with the fruits of their love, if any there is,) according to his means and ability, after the co-partnership is dissolved, or until the woman is re-married, and also provide for the children, until they are able to support themselves Neither should a man, in case of such dissolution, have any claim or control over the property which the woman possessed at the time of her marriage, or any that might be inherited by her at a subsequent period.

I will now briefly glance at the laws pertaining to seductions. Your lexicographers define the word 'Seduce' thus: "To corrupt; to lead astray;" but in Holy Writ we read that the man "Samson," while talking with the "Philistines" respecting his heifer, charged them with having led her astray, and by so doing they had discovered where his great strength lay. Now as the heifer he spoke of could lay but little claims to virtue or morality, as she, like many of the present day, entertained strangers during the absence of her lord, and as it is impossible to corrupt a thing that is already corrupted, I have sometimes thought that a substantive could be coined, and introduced into the English language, which would be more comprehensive than that word as it is now used and understood. Be that as it may, I am of opinion that the most stringent laws now in existence, with their penalties connected, are altogether too loose, and too light, to reach the case of a man who coolly and deliberately wins the affections of a woman, for the purpose of robbing her of her virtue, and then deserting her; but the great trouble is that the wisest-headed Legislature that ever framed a law has not been able to adopt, nay, even conceive a plan whereby a Judge or Jury, when a case of seduction is brought before them for adjudication, can tell for a certainty which of the parties are at fault. In other words, they cannot discover which of the twain were seduced. Reasonable and upright dispensers of the law will examine cases of this kind with great care, (sometimes they will pry and peep in a little farther than they ought to,) but they will generally render a verdict in favor of the woman, because her evidence must be admitted, while that of the man is thrown out entirely.

It is a very singular fact, that in nine cases out of ten, where men are charged with the crime of seduction, you will find the accused are men who are possessed of property, to a greater or less amount. How happens this, when the fact is well known that the proportion of wealthy men, compared with those of the laborıng clas ses, do not average one to six ?

Why is it that you rarely find a poor man brought up on the charge of seduction? If the reasons are not obvious to every reader, they must examine into the subject themselves, for I shall not attempt to explain them.

My own impressions are, that in two cases out of three, where men are prosecuted and arraigned for offences of this kind, especially those who are possessed of a large amount of worldly goods, I say, in two cases out of three, the "woman" is the seducer, not the man; and it always appears that these poor, confiding, and abused females, who have been thus wickedly led astray, and injured in their reputation, fair name and fame, will generally claim damages to the amount of fifteen or twenty thousand dollars, and if the Jury award them as many hundreds, they will go on their way rejoicing, having received

> "A balm for every wound,
> A cordial for their fears."

If I am correct in these premises, in asserting my belief boldly, and only reiterating the sentiments of thousands who have more carefully examined the subject than I have, would it not be well for our Judges and Jurors to examine more carefully than they do each and every case of this kind that is brought before them, and instead of being influenced by the sobs and tears of some fair (perhaps frail) Dulcinea, who has been instructed how to play her part by the lawyer who manages her case, and who is to receive a portion of the spoils, if any is awarded; to weigh carefully every part of the evidence, and give a wide margin to a large portion of it.

I could cite many cases that have come under my own observation, and which would demonstrate the fact that oftentimes it is the man who is seduced, and not the woman. To do this would not be politic or judicious, as no one would be benefitted by their perusal. I will, however, allude to one, and one only, and then I shall drop the subject.

A young man, who belongs to, and was doing business in a city near Boston, became enamoured of a gay, dashing young woman, who occasionally visited the house of one of his friends. She and all her relatives were poorer than church mice. while he was supposed to be worth twenty or thirty thousand dollars. This cunning, calculating woman used every artifice, and left no stone unturned, to inveigle him, and draw him onward to the first fatal step, which, if once taken, cannot be retraced, and often leads to perdition. He listened to the song of the siren, until the fatal step was taken.

When this cunning woman informed him that she was ruined, and that there was no alternative between what a priest or Justice of the Peace could perform, or an *ex-*

pose to the world, and an application for redress in a court of law. The young man chose the former, after having offered the vixen three thousand dollars if she would give up all claims against him. This being refused, a priest was called, and the marriage ceremony performed.

Shortly after the marriage, the young man, who had invested largely in provisions, which he had shipped to California, and which on their arrival there were sold under the auctioneer's hammer for a mere song, scarcely amounting to enough to pay the freight, together with the failure of some friends whose notes he had endorsed, was driven into chancery by his creditors, and his house, horse, and rich furniture, were disposed of by the assignee.

When his loving spouse discovered how matters stood, her wrath and fury knew no bounds. She asseverated to her husband's friends, relatives and creditors, that he had put his property (or a portion of it) out of his hands, and that the residue had been squandered away at the gaming-table, and in bar-rooms; (it may be proper to add that the young man never saw the interior of a gaming-room in his life, and never played dice or cards even for the amount of one penny. When this model of a wife found that everything was irrevocably lost, she concocted a plan whereby to retrieve their fallen fortunes. She proposed to her husband the plan of inviting to the house an old wealthy merchant, who had, as she averred, often looked upon her with lecherous eyes, and entrapping him, while he was closeted with her in her chamber.

The husband was thunder-struck at this proposition. He well knew that his wife was a shrew, but never imagined that she would prostitute herself for gain. He gathered up some papers, and a few trinkets which were valuable to him, and left the house, to return no more. The wife is now a courtezan, while the husband is in one of our western cities, and by close attention to business is trying to regain the position which he once held in society.

In this case, as well as in others near akin to it, which I could chronicle, and should, if I thought the world would be advantaged thereby. I would in all candor ask, which of the parties were seduced? Which the seducer? Let not the reader say that this may be all true, but it is an isolated case, and the young man who marries without fully informing himself of the previous character and proclivities of the woman with whom he intends to unite, is not much better than a fool; and if one who has come to the years of discretion allows his passions to predominate, and with open eyes walks upon the brink of a precipice from which thousands have been hurled before. If he falls into the yawning gulf, and is carried down the stream, beyond the reach of human aid, there is no one to blame but himself. Is this always so? Where will you find the person, whose testimony is to be relied upon. You will in such a case as I have cited; inform either of the parties respecting what they may know of their character, or moral worth? If they make an assertion which is founded in truth, but which they cannot prove, respecting the character of any person who is not so notoriously bad that the world looks upon them as vile, they lay themselves liable to be brought up in a suit of slander, and be subjected to heavy penalties. Hundreds of innocent men have suffered by being unjustly charged with the crime of seduction, and obliged to pay large amounts of money, in the form of fines and damages, while hundreds of females have suffered still more, when they have been decoyed, and led from the path of rectitude and virtue, by libertines and designing villains, who are fit subjects for the Penitentiary or gibbet, and who, instead of being driven without the pale of society, are tolerated, flattered, and their company courted, by females who have a reputation to maintain, and are well aware of the character of these despicable villains. So much has been said and written on this subject, that it appears almost impossible to introduce anything new, and I have given the reader my views on it, in the briefest possible manner.

I will now turn to another subject, or, I should say,

a subject and crime, akin to this, and that is the commission of the crime of "Rape."

I am of the belief that the man (or the brute in the form of a man,) who is guilty of committing this crime, should be put out of existence, if his guilt is fairly proved, in as summary manner as would be a rabid dog, for the very good reason that he is equally, perhaps ten times more dangerous than the four footed animal. The one follows the instincts of nature, and the other does no more, or less; but the one has nothing but instinct to govern him, while the other is supposed to be endowed with reasoning faculties, and an immortal soul. The one is considered dangerous, and is always quickly dispatched, without the assistance of Judge or Jury; the other is ten-fold more dangerous, because the law requires that the biped who is guilty of this offence shall have the advantage of a fair trial, and in nine cases out of ten goes clear, while the animal, unpossessed of reasoning faculties, is dispatched at once.

When the laws in this section of the country consigned a man to the gallows for committing the crime of rape, it was almost impossible to convict a man of the crime, however clear and positive the proofs may have been, as elicited in the trial, because the Jurors were unwilling to consign a man to a felon's death, where they were satisfied that the offender was more an object of pity than of vengeance. The last execution which took place in the State of Massachusetts, which was many years ago, (I do not recollect the time or date,) was so strongly deprecated by the majority of the community, that the laws pertaining to this crime were altered, and imprisonment for life was substituted for the death penalty. I well remember that in this case, the female, who was at the time of the trial supposed to be a virtuous woman, was afterwards shown to be a prostitute of the worst description.

The great lawgiver to the Israelites appears to have understood this subject far better than the lawgivers of the present day, although he overlooked, or perhaps imagined it impossible for a man to commit the crime upon a child. I can only account for this by supposing that even among that ignorant and oppressed people which he led forth out of the land of Egypt, there were none found so vile and debased as to be guilty of this enormity.

I think every reasonable person will agree with me when I say, that the quicker a man who is guilty of the commission of this crime, and convicted of the same, is put out of the world, the better it will be for the interest of the community at large; but I presume there are hundreds who will not favor my belief, when I say that there have been many executed, and many more imprisoned, charged with the commission of this crime, who were guiltless, or, in other words, not entirely at fault, who have suffered unjustly, while this tyrannical law was in force.

I hardly believe such a thing to be possible as the commission of the crime of rape upon an adult female, who is in perfect possession of health, and those faculties which a benign and beneficent Creator has bestowed upon all His children. In His all-wise power He has given to every creature that exists suitable means of defending themselves, and more especially to the creature man. And I am slow to believe that the female, whether it be of the human or animal species, is not endowed with sufficient strength and power to resist all amatory advances of the opposite sex, after they have come to the years of maturity. I know many will differ from me in this opinion, and say I am entirely wrong; nevertheless, they cannot alter my belief. In the case of a child, I grant that this is far different. To those brutes (and there are many that exist who would, and do commit such crimes upon them,) I should say that the punishment awarded by the Chinese laws to the parricide, would be altogether too mild; but when you talk to me of a female in full feather, who meets one of the opposite sex, single handed and alone, who cannot defend herself (unless she is drugged or injured) from any and every assault of this kind, I shall get information that I have yet to learn.

During the reign of Queen Elizabeth, a young officer

in the army was charged, tried and convicted of the crime of rape, and the sentence of death had been pronounced upon him. The death-warrant was passed in for Her Majesty's signature. When the good, or bad Queen, (I care not which you call her,) took up the paper, after having dipped her pen into the inkstand, she turned to one of her Prime Ministers, and asked :

" How old was the child upon whom this offence was committed ?"

The Minister smiled, as he replied :

" I think, your Majesty, that the woman is about thirty years of age."

" And what is the age of the condemned man ?" returned the Queen.

" Judging from his appearance, I should think he was twenty-four or five years of age," was the reply.

The Queen threw the death-warrant upon her table, as she remarked :

" Let this interesting couple be brought before me; I wish to see both parties, before the man is executed."

The day following, the Queen convened her Counsellors, and the injured woman was brought before them.

The Queen, who had examined the reports of the evidence in the case, asked the woman whether she of her own free will entered the complaint against the convicted party, or whether it was done at the instigation of others.

The woman frankly acknowledged that her husband obliged her to enter the complaint, asseverating, at the same time, that in the rendition of her testimony she had adhered strictly to the truth.

"If you were a single woman, and the convicted man should offer to atone for his crime by marrying you, would you consent to it?"

"Most certainly, your Majesty," was the reply.

"So I supposed," returned the Queen; "and I therefore grant a full pardon to the accused, and order that he be immediately reinstated into his office in the army, and that the woman be suffered to depart."

This example goes to show that wherever the death penalty follows the conviction of the crime of rape, men may suffer when they are not alone at fault, and that the old English Queen understood human nature much better than did some of her law-givers and law-dispensers.

When that time arrives (I fear it is far distant) when laws are enacted which will operate equally upon all classes of people; when men who frame laws legislate for the benefit of the whole, and not for the advantage of a few; then will the world become honest, and men will learn to "fear God, and keep his commandments, for this is the whole duty of man."

One-half of the misery, vice and crime which abounds at the present day, is attributable to parents, who do not guard their children carefully in early life, and point out to them the temptations, snares, and besetting sins which constantly surround them. The father who sends his sons to school, and compels them to attend divine worship on the Sabbath, imagines that he has done his whole duty, and all that can be required of him; and the mother who strives to give her daughters what is called a genteel education, failing to instruct them in those matters which are so necessary to their future well-being, sees with sorrow and regret her error, when it is too late.

One of the most curious and novel cases which we have on record, is that of a boy between eight and nine years of age, who was charged with, and indicted by the Grand Jury of the County of Suffolk, Massachusetts, for committing the crime of rape. When the child was brought into court, and arraigned at the Bar, the Judge looked at him with astonishment, and the Jury, equally astonished, looked at the Judge.

After a few moments consideration, the Judge inquired of the County Attorney whether he knew the age of the child, when the indictment was found.

"I knew it was a minor, your Honor, but I did not know that he was an infant."

"I am at a loss to know what to do with him," quoth the Judge.

The attorney replied:

"I am not much of a physician, but if I advised in the case, I should recommend twenty-five or thirty drops of the oil of birch, skilfully applied, by an experienced hand, together with very plain diet, until the patient has entirely recovered, and I think that the mother of the child, if he has one living, would be the proper person to appoint as nurse."

The Judge agreeing with the County Attorney in his opinion, ordered the precocious young gentleman to be set at liberty.

It may not be amiss to add, that the female upon whom the assault was alleged to have been committed, was two or three years older than the boy, and as the complaint set forth that the assailant was a minor, the County Attorney and Grand Jury were led to suppose that he was from fifteen to twenty years of age.

Cases like this do not often occur, but the Grand Jury often put too much dependance on the State's Attorney, and take it for granted that he has carefully investigated every case, before it is brought before them.

I am well aware that there are many who will peruse these pages, who do, and will, differ from me in my views and opinions, not only respecting the laws pertaining to divorce, seduction, and rape, but also with regard to other laws, as I have glanced at them. But let all such remember that I will go as fast and as far in supporting all judicious laws, when they are properly administered, as any other person in the community.

Before I leave this subject I will remark that many people believe (I certainly agree with them,) that in every city where there is a Police or Recorder's court established, an honest and competent man, who is well versed in law, should be appointed and paid by the State to defend those who are arraigned for criminal offences, who have not the means to procure the services of an attorney. At any rate, this is an experiment which is worth a trial, because if it did not operate successfully, it could be discontinued. Such a plan would further the ends of justice, instead of retarding its course, and at the same time give to to the person who is charged with committing crime, and, as is often the case, convicted, when in truth they were guilty of the crime of poverty, and that alone; to such it would give some opportunities for a defence, which otherwise they cannot have.

This subject is worth the consideration of those philanthropic individuals who would relieve the miseries of the poor and distressed.

CHAPTER XIV.

The miseries which men suffer by running in debt—The evil results of the same—The Debtor always a Slave to the Creditor—The way young men usually commence business, and fail—The Ruffian Creditor and Exasperated Debtor—The Creditor sometimes more to blame than the Debtor—The "Betterment Law," The abused Legislature of 1855—Just and judicious laws enacted by them—Two extreme cases where persons were imprisoned for debt—Sketch of John Augustus, the Philanthropist—Sketch of William D. Eaton—Hinman Meredith, the man who has transacted business for twenty-five years, to the amount of fifteen millions of dollars, and never saw the interior of a Court Room, &c.

As I have briefly given my views and opinions of the debt and credit system, as it now exists, sanctioned by law, it may be considered superfluous to refer to the subject again; but as this is the fountain-head and source of litigation, and as a portion of mankind prey upon the other part, by leading them into law-suits which could easily be avoided, too much cannot be said or written on the subject, if what is said or written, tends in the slightest degree to enlighten those who are blindly disposed to seek redress in our courts of law, for any and every real, or supposed grievance.

How true the maxim: "The debtor is always the slave of the creditor." The moment that a man becomes indebted to his fellow-man, no matter whether he is friend or foe, or what the amount of his indebtedness may be, if he cannot meet his payments at the time they become due, from that moment the debtor becomes the slave, and pliant, cringing tool of the creditor. In fact, the debtor becomes the property of the creditor, both his body and boots. If the debtor is a man, (all are not men who bear the human form,) he scarcely dares to go into a clothing store, and purchase a suit of apparel, lest his creditor may be looking over his shoulder, ready to shout in his ears: "Pay me what thou owest!" Or if some kind friend should trust him for the garments, or give them to him, (which would amount to one and the same thing,) the poor debtor dare not put them on and wear them, lest he should meet one of his creditors, who would point him out to the crowd, and say:

"Look at that finished rascal! he owes me a sum of money, honestly due, which he will not pay, while he walks round wearing a better suit of clothes than I can possibly afford to."

The poor debtor cannot even attend divine worship on the Sabbath, without being pointed out to the congregation, if he hires a convenient and comfortable seat, without being told he had better sit in one of the pews designed for the poor and indigent, until such time as he can pay his honest debts, If the poor debtor is invited by a friend to visit the theatre, opera-house, or a public levee or dinner, it often happens that he will not accept, although the entertainment would not cost him a groat; he dreads the idea of meeting some creditor, who will boldly confront him, and make his ears tingle, as he listens to some exclamations like these :

"Well, Mr. B., you can find money enough to pay two or three dollars for an opera ticket, but can't cancel that little bill that's been standing for a long time."

Or if the debtor happens to be engaged in conversation with some of his female friends, attempting to make himself as agreeable as possible, it would be no music in his ears to hear some malicious creditor remark to some others in the company, something like this :

"Mr. B—— looks first-rate, this evening, with my coat and pantaloons on."

Wherever the debtor may go, he is sure to be dogged about, in some form or another, by the creditor. He will meet him at the door of his dwelling, at early dawn, at noon, in the street, as he returns to and from his meals, in fact, anywhere and everywhere that the unfortunate victim may be, the cry is :

"Sir, can you pay that little bill ?"

The debtor, comparatively an honest man, is obliged to resort to all sorts of trickery, prevarication and falsehood, to temporarily escape from, and rid himself of, the importunities of the creditor, who is his master, and who will follow him, watching every movement, until every farthing is paid, or the death of the poor insolvent debtor cancels the bond.

If an ambitious, enterprising young man, has, by months and years of toil, accumulated a few hundred dollars, and undertakes to start in business for himself, he is apt to conclude that it is necessary for him to obtain a certain amount of credit, otherwise he cannot compete with those who are possessed of more means than himself. The wholesale dealer, after making the necessary investigation respecting the young man's business habits, his associates, &c., will give him credit to twice the amount of his real capital; but if he is a shrewd merchant, he will so manage that in case the young man should not succeed in business, he himself would lose nothing, even if other creditors should suffer. Merchants number two, three, four, and so on, when they find that the young man's credit is good with merchant number one, are also ready to give him credit, and importune him to trade with them, which in nine cases out of ten he will readily do. In the first place, the young merchant was the slave of only one man; now he has four or five masters, and he must obey the directions of all of them. If he steals and pockets the entire proceeds of all their goods with which he has been entrusted, he is called smart; but if he has made wrong calculations, and bought goods which have depreciated in value while upon his hands, and after he has taken a careful account of stock, he finds that he cannot meet all his liabilities, and delivers it up for the benefit of his creditors, he is spoken of as one totally unfit for business, and not to be trusted under any consideration.

As a general thing, we find that men who are new beginners in trade, attach but little importance to the small debts and liabilities which they contract, however shrewd and active they may be in collecting bills due to them. They would, under no circumstances, if they could possibly avoid it, allow a note of one hundred dollars, held against them, to be protested, but the small bills of the butcher, the baker, and the washerwoman, they will allow to remain unpaid, and those persons who are least able to bear the loss of a dollar, are oftentimes the greatest losers by those who live for a time upon the credit system, and when they fail, injure those who have always benefitted them.

It is said by some who are supposed to thoroughly understand the subject, that the proportion of those who commence business for themselves, in the mercantile community, and succeed, is about eleven per cent. If this calculation is correct, (and I am inclined to believe it is,) eighty-nine persons out of the hundred, among merchants and traders of every description, are declared insolvent within the average space of ten years.

Occasionally you will find a man, merchant, or trader, who will give credit, and seldom lose any of his debts, while another, placed in the same situation, would find it impossible to collect the amounts, or any portion thereof, from the same debtors. This is easily accounted for. In the first case, the creditor well understands human nature, he knows how to manage his customers, and will so treat with them, that he will at once obtain their good will, and make the debtor feel that he is under some obligations to the creditor, outside and beyond his indebtedness. How often do we hear the remark from those who have been unfortunate, and failed in business: "Mr. So and So shall be paid, if no other person ever receives a cent;" and this, too, when the creditor spoken of is in no way connected with the debtor, either by ties of blood or friendship.

In the other case, the creditor who does not understand human nature, will become exasperated when he finds that he cannot collect his just dues at the proper time, and instead of being conciliatory in his language and demeanor, towards the debtor, will be harsh and abusive. This is not, nor never was, the way to win. The debtor may have the best intentions, and would not, perhaps, for his right hand, wrong the creditor out of a farthing; but the latter has, by his abuse and insults, placed a great gulf between himself and his debtor, over which neither of them will pass, and the debtor would rather submit to the tortures of the thumb-screws and rack, than to pay one penny of the debt which he acknowledges is justly and fairly due.

On one occasion, as I was passing through the principal thoroughfare of New York city, in company with a friend, when we were both brought to a sudden halt by a rough-looking, hard visaged mechanic, who accosted my friend, and with oaths averred that if he did not pay him the amount of a bill which he claimed against him, he would, within one week from that day, pound him to a jelly.

After we had separated from the ruffian creditor, my companion informed me that he was indebted to the man to the amount of fifty or sixty dollars, but being very much embarrassed himself, at the time the bill became due, he was obliged to keep him out of his money for two or three months; but he had made arrangements whereby he could cancel this, and a few other liabilities of the same nature, and intended to pay the man the following day; but now, said he, "I shall not pay him until he comes and apologizes for the rude manner in which he has insulted me."

We see cases like this occurring every day, where men who cannot meet the just demands of their creditors at the very time they should be adjusted, will, after having been abused, and threatened with law-suits, and prison bars and bolts, become exasperated, and either not settle the claim at all, or compel the creditor to expend two dollars for every one which he collects of them.

Men often become involved, and run deeply into debt, when the creditor is more in fault than the debtor.

If a person is supposed to be solvent, and has the reputation of being attentive to business, he is often cajoled and urged by shrewd tradesmen to purchase goods which he does not really need, and which he would not purchase if he was obliged to pay for them, cash in hand, at the time of their delivery; but the trader says: "Pay for them whenever you please; I'm in no hurry," &c. But pay-day will come, and the easy man is brought to a full realization of the fact, when he finds that a sheriff has taken possession of his house or store.

There is one subject more to which I will call the attention of the reader, and that is the operation of a law which was enacted by the Massachusetts Legislature, several years ago, (I cannot recall to my mind the exact date,) called the "Betterment Law." My reason for noticing this law, is, that at the time of its enactment, the middling and lower classes of the community were told (and most of them believed it,) that it was passed expressly for their benefit. After the Revolutionary War, large tracts of land, in every part of the State, were deserted by their lawful proprietors, and there was no records left to show to whom they rightfully belonged. Among the poorer class there were many who settled upon these grounds, built small tenements, and supposed that after the term of twenty years had elapsed, if the rightful owner did not come to claim the property, it would revert to them, which indeed it would; but if within that space of time a legal claimant should appear, they must be driven out of possession, and have no claim whatever upon them, for the "betterments," or improvements which they had made.

The poor man believed that this law was passed expressly for *his* benefit, while those who enacted the law, framed it expressly for their *own*. Large tracts of valuable land, in the western section of what is now the city of Boston, and in other portions of the State, were immediately taken up by those immaculate law-givers, (or some of their friends,) and the "betterments," as these cunning financiers had arranged the law, amounted to twice the original worth of the land. When one of the real owners, their assignees, heirs, or assigns, came forward to prove and claim the property which rightfully belonged to them, the "betterments" so far exceeded what they supposed to be their real value, that most of them relinquished their claims, rather than to pay the amount demanded.

Probably there are not a dozen men, who now own or possess real estate, which is at the present time considered very valuable, in the western section of the city of Boston, who have a free and clear right and title to the land on which their buildings stand, and perhaps not one fiftieth part of them know who the true owners are or were.

The much abused Legislature of Massachusetts, in the year 1855, did enact some laws which were, in deed and in truth, judicious, and long needed, and there were many men attached to that Legislature who deserve the lasting praise and gratitude of their constituents.

One of these enactments I will mention; that is, the "Homestead Bill," which provides for every man, the right to hold, exempt from legal attachment, a shelter for himself and family. A wife or child should never be made to suffer for the sins or misfortunes of the husband and father, and it is a relic of a barbarous age, that gave the creditor such power over the poor debtor, as would allow him to drive forth the family of an unfortunate man, and take possession of their domicil, leaving them to buffet with the cold storm and wintry blast, or apply to the Alms-house for relief. We have had too much of this, altogether, in the State where first landed the Pilgrim Fathers, and where the first blood was shed in defence of American liberties.

This Legislature also abolished the law of imprisonment for debt, which had long remained upon our Statute Books, a lasting memorial of shame and disgrace. Thousands have suffered unjustly, under this law, by being taken from their work-shops and their families, and incarcerated in prison cells, because they could not pay just (sometimes unjust) claims which were held against them. Before the abolition of this law, the creditor was always obliged to pay the board of the debtor, while he was confined within the prison walls. Start not, nor be astonished, kind reader, when I tell you that I have the evidence and the proof to show that men have been incarcerated in Leverett Street Jail, in the city of Boston, for non-payment of a small sum of money, without any possible means of escape, while the creditor has placed the price of their liberation—at what? (I shudder while I record the fact;) the prostitution of the wife or daughter of the unfortunate debtor!

> "Can such things be, and overcome us like a summer's cloud,
> Without our special wonder?"

All this is true; aye, more, the thousandth part of the iniquities which have been practiced under this abominable law, not only in Massachusetts, but in every section of the country, where this law was tolerated, would, if they were recorded, make the angels weep tears of blood.

I have known cases (isolated, I grant,) where a debtor rather courted the prison than otherwise, and by harsh language and defiant looks, drove the creditor to take advantage of the law, and imprison him. I will cite two cases, both of which are extreme, in illustration.

I knew a case of a young man who had received a liberal education, and who possessed all those moral principles that are requisite to place a man high in the estimation of the community. It might, however, be said of him, as was said of one of old: "One thing thou lackest;" that is, knowledge of business, and the character of mankind.

This worthy young gentleman (by the advice of his friends) commenced business in the city of Boston, but was soon obliged to relinquish it, because he could not make his payments when they became due. After he had been "ousted" from his store, one of his creditors, more opportune than others in their demands, caused him to be arrested, and put in durance vile. The amount due this creditor was *ten dollars and seventy cents!* At the time of his incarceration he had not money enough in his pocket (or elsewhere) to pay for the conveyance of a letter to any of his friends. He was confined more than forty-eight hours before he was liberated, and when the creditor was upbraided for this mean and contemptible act, his reply was:

"The rascal wears as good clothes as I do, and could pay the bill, if he felt disposed."

In this case I know that the young man had had abundant opportunities to defraud and swindle many persons out of large amounts, without the possibility of detection.

As the law is now obselete in every State where the majority of the citizens believe in those doctrines inculcated by the meek and lowly Nazarene, it is useless to treat farther on this subject; and lest I should entirely forget and overlook it, I will give sketches of distinguished individuals which were omitted in a previous chapter.

Among the notables who have been in and about the Boston Court House for the past twelve years, few are better known than the man John Augustus. That this man has done much good, since he entered upon his career as a Philanthropist, no one who knows anything of the subject can for a moment doubt. Many persons are of the opinion that for a few years past Mr. Augustus has done more harm than good, by bailing those who are arraigned before the courts for the commission of crimes that deserve, and should receive severe punishment, and it is said that rogues have been allowed to escape through the interposition of this man.

There may be a few cases where this gentleman's philanthropy (or whatever else you please to term it,) has so far out run good judgment and discretion, that it may have led him to interfere, where strict justice would demand that the law should take its course. If the facts respecting such matters were fully known, methinks the public would find that where one truly guilty individual has escaped, by and with the aid of John Augustus, ten

JOHN AUGUSTUS.

(See Page 282.)

have been suffered to go at large by the connivance and direct assistance of police officers.

Mr. Augustus commenced his career as a Philanthropist in 1841, in the Police Court of Boston, by bailing a man who was charged with the offence of being a common drunkard. The following year he bailed seventeen persons, all of whom were arraigned for the same offence. From that time down to the present he has continued in the laudable enterprise, and has bailed nearly five thousand people charged with this offence. Now if one out of five of this number has been reclaimed, by his interposition in their behalf, surely he has been a benefactor of mankind, and has not lived in vain.

There is one thing certainly that is praiseworthy in the character of John Augustus, and that is, he will never quarrel with any person, on account of their political opinions or religious belief; neither will he express his own, even when urged to do so. By pursuing this course, he is, like the Apostle Paul, enabled to make himself "all things to all men," believing that by so doing he can "*save some.*"

There are but few men to be found, who would, if they had been placed in precisely his situation, stood the ordeal of public opinion for fourteen years, and retained the good opinion of those who stand high in the community, as the most charitable and beneficent citizens. I believe that whenever and wherever he has made mistakes, in his impetuous zeal in laboring for the good of others, it has been the fault of the head, and not the heart.

The engraving of Mr. Augustus, which may be found in this work, is a tolerably fair representatton of the man, although not so correct as it should be.

WILLIAM D. EATON.

This Police Officer, whose portrait will be found within the pages of this book, is a man extensively known. He has been connected with the Police Department of Boston for ten or eleven years.

In the year 1847, Mr. Eaton was appointed Deputy City Marshal of Boston, and after the office of "City Marshal" was abolished, and a Chief of Police established in its stead, Mr. Eaton received the appointment of Deputy Chief, which office he held for two years. He was then transferred to the position which he now holds, viz.: Captain of Police Station, in District No. 4.

As a thief-catcher, and rogue-detector, Mr. E. has but few equals, perhaps no superiors.

I have been told that Mr. Eaton is a very humane man, and is always ready to render all the assistance in his power to relieve the needy and suffering. It is said that in the year 1850, when the cholera visited the city of Boston, there was no person who more assiduously labored to relieve wants and sufferings of the sick, and provide for those who were left widows and orphans, than he was, and there were but few who received so little commendation at the time for valuable services rendered.

I regret that space will not allow me to give a more extended notice of this well-known officer.

HINMAN MEREDITH, ESQ.,

The reader of these pages will naturally inquire why the author of a work like this, should introduce one who knows nothing of Courts, Judges, Attornies, Police Officers, Coroners, Justices of the Peace, Recorders, Court Reporters, or other *attachees* of civil or criminal courts, either in this country, or in the land that gave him birth.

The question is very easily answered: For the very reason that Mr. Meredith has, by both precept and example, demonstrated the fact that a man can transact business, and have dealings with his fellow men, without litigation.

Perhaps it would be impossible to find another man in the United States, who has done business to the same amount, commencing, as he did, some twenty-three years ago, with a few hard earned sovereigns in his pocket, and accumulating a little, year by year, until he reached the acme of trade, and compete with those who are styled merchant princes, without ever having feed a lawyer, looked into the interior of a court-room, under any circumstances, with no personal knowledge, practically applied, of ever having sued or complained of a man, in any case at law. Nor did he ever have an Attorney's letter directed to him, which commenced thus :

"A demand has been left at my office, against you, for collection," &c., &c.

Mr. M. is an eccentric and unostentatious man. He never gave a note of hand, nor will he take one, even should it be endorsed by the President of every Bank in the United States.

I trust, for the reasons already mentioned, the reader will be perfectly satisfied with my explanation of the why's and wherefore's, in this matter.

Hinman Meredith was born in Algerkirk, England, some fifty-two years ago. He came to this country in the year 1833, and commenced business as a retail West India goods dealer, in a small store, on Washington street, Boston. He brought with him a few dollars. He would not accept proffered credit from any man, neither would he extend credit to any man. Every article brought into his store was paid for in ready cash, and every purchaser was required to adhere to his rule, most strictly and religiously.

It is not well to shower fulsome praise or laudations upon any man, while he is living, therefore I shall only speak of Mr. M. as he is spoken of by others.

It is said that he is kind hearted, affable and generous, in all the social relations of life, a sincere open-hearted, and true friend to all who are so fortunate as to become intimately acquainted with him. In matters of business he is scrupulously exact, whether in selling a pound of tea, or a thousand boxes of sugar.

The eccentricities and peculiarities of Mr. M. are always instantly noticed by an observing stranger, the moment he comes in contact with him. These, we believe, are partially innate, but the force of habit may have done much to augment them.

Although Mr. M. was born in England, he is a true republican. He never meddles with politics, never expresses any opinions with regard to party or sects, but ever has been diligent in business, and has set an example for the young men of the present day, which, if they would follow, would certainly lead them to wealth and prosperity. He has clearly shown that a man can accumulate riches without injuring his neighbors. That to avoid litigations, and law quarrels, with all their concomitants, is the only safe course for a business man to pursue. We know full well that Mr. M. has many times and oft relieved the sufferings of the worthy poor and distressed, always doing it by stealth, when no reporter was near, or printing-press ready to blazon the deed to the world. He has quietly made deposits in that Bank where you get no written receipt, but where every farthing is credited in the ledger kept above.

I find that I must bring these sketches to a close,

having devoted more time and space to the subject than I intended at its commencement. The little curly-headed devil, with hands and face smutched with printer's ink, will no longer come to my chamber at early dawn, and poke his roguish phiz inside the half-open door, crying out: "Please, sir, we want copy." No longer will the gentlemanly proprietor of the stereotype foundry call upon me, with some half a dozen sheets of unintelligible manuscript, that could not be deciphered, and insist upon knowing the name of the person who invented that style of hieroglyphics. No longer will my venerable Uncle Zeb perplex and annoy me, because every word and line written is not in exact accordance with his old fashioned whims and notions; and as I no longer intend to trouble the reader on this subject, I will

DROP THE VEIL.

www.ingramcontent.com/pod-product-compliance
Lightning Source LLC
LaVergne TN
LVHW010211110826
845151LV00004B/1049
* 9 7 8 1 4 2 5 5 2 8 6 5 2 *